M000202197

THE HUMILITY AND SUFFERING OF GOD

THE HUMILITY AND SUFFERING OF GOD

by Francois Varillon

Translated by Nelly Marans

ALBA · HOUSE   NEW · YORK

SOCIETY OF ST. PAUL, 2187 VICTORY BLVD., STATEN ISLAND, NEW YORK 10314

ACKNOWLEDGMENTS

The quotations from Scripture are all taken from the English text of The Jerusalem Bible.

The quotation from St. John of the Cross was taken from the English translation of E. Allison Peers. The quotations from Thomas Aquinas were taken from the Aquinas Reader *(Doubleday, Image Books) by Mary T. Clark.*

All other quotations were translated from French into English by the translator herself.

Library of Congress Cataloging in Publication Data

Varillon, François, 1905—
  The humility and suffering of God.

  Translation of: L'humilité de Dieu, and La Souffrance de Dieu.
    1. God. 2. Suffering of God. I. Varillon, François, 1905— . Souffrance de Dieu. English. 1983. II. Title.
  BT102.V3713   1983   231   83-2724
  ISBN 0-8189-0448-8

This book was originally published by Editions du Centurion, Paris, under the title *L'humilité de Dieu*, 1974 and *La Souffrance de Dieu*, 1975.

Imprimatur (French Edition)
† *E. Berrar*
Paris, 1974, 1975

TABLE OF CONTENTS

PART I
THE HUMILITY OF GOD

PART II
THE SUFFERING OF GOD

Part I
THE HUMILITY OF GOD

The Virtue Called Humility
is Deep-rooted in the Deity

MEISTER ECKHART

Chapter One

DOGMATIC CONSIDERATIONS

My purpose in writing this book is such that the use of "I" has to be considered as less detestable than its absence would be. The absence of "I" is often a paradoxical lack of modesty. Whoever omits it has pretenses of magisterial affirmation. Conversely, the presence of "I" on the foreground and even in closeup, shows that one can communicate with simplicity a mixture of what can be expressed in all security—the faith of the Church—and of what can be uttered less securely: the value and suitability of an emphasis. Here: the humility of God.

This is an emphasis, a stress. *I* believe that *I* can say: God is humble. When *I* pray, I talk to one who is humbler than I am. When *I* confess my sin, I am asking the forgiveness of one who is humbler than I am. If God were not humble, *I* would hesitate to describe him as infinitely loving. This aspect of the mystery is that which convinces *me*, being what I am, that the revelation is true. Not that other aspects are being excluded, but this particular one convinces me with a more intimate and irrefutable power.

Recently, when Father Auguste Valensin entitled a book *Autour de ma foi* (Around My Faith), his deliberate use of the possessive did not imply that the author was being stand-offish with regard to faith, but that he chose to stress the reasons for believing that were "strong" for him, to the extent, as he put it, that he had to give in to them. Even if others were to find them weak and unworthy to be preferred! In the same way, all due allowances being made, I choose to express my motivations in these difficult times, to utter that which in me resists ideological pressures, extreme frenzies, superficial unrest, fashion. That which impels me to talk about God to my contemporaries, and I will go so far as to say: to talk only about him.

Freely using this "I," I shall write in a discontinuous manner, without the rigidity of a logical composition. I shall make free to repeat myself, though my repetitions are on various planes and highlighted in diverse ways and cannot be, properly speaking, seen as mere reiterations. For instance, talking about God, the meaning of the word *humility* can only be unveiled little by little unless one were to define it outside of experience, as lived or described. The blank remaining on the paper which Claudel deemed necessary to a poem is not without religious efficacy in ordinary prose: it enables adoration to breath in the spaces of the argumentation or even up to its heart. A talk to God within a talk about God! Or silence to make the discourse bearable.

And since poets, artists, writers—at least those who have been capable of bringing the quality of their being to a flowing purity—are usually the companions of my work and even of my prayer, I see no reason for parting from them when I am going to share with others that which they have contributed to my development.

There are two equally irritating attitudes: the first one excludes questioning, hence uneasiness, from religion; the other is systematically looking for both.

Many are those who imagine that the Church has an answer for everything, and at any time. It would be enough for the theologian to reach out quickly into a treasure trove of irrefutable arguments in order to fill up the cracks that have appeared in the bulwark of security. Let him give in to such naive entreaties, and authority will lose what will be gained by a strengthened suspicion.

On the other hand, one finds people who are obsessed with questioning. Being alert to what is new and plentiful in the world, they run the risk of knowing nothing about the Christian Tradition except its weakest moments, which might well be its most recent ones. They have little tolerance for what they have been taught. They remember what courses in apologetics used to be in the first third of this century.

Periods of weakness can only be judged in their own context. And it is the memory that provides the context. If one confuses attachment to the past for its own sake with tradition, memory becomes hateful, and one will believe himself to be a prophet by the simple process of cancelling that which was before he was, by questioning from scratch. Heritage is totally rejected because it is viewed as alienating, and all norms are erased. What could have been stimulating collapses in delusion. I want to keep uneasiness alive so that my faith may grow and become purified. But I will be careful, as Péguy said, "not to neglect organic memory . . . living memory, or to put it more simply—because its very name is self-sufficient—memory."

When I reread the famous lecture given by Karl Barth in 1956 on *l'Humanité de Dieu* (The Humanity of God), I admire its tone. What dignity, what calm! It is *recantation* but not *cancellation.* To say in a better way what has already been said, to say it at last in the right way, without breaking away from tradition, though while admitting that critical attitudes and positions are generally only partially true. Neither impatience nor uproar, but as Plato put it when talking about the geometer: the silent forward thrust of a river of oil. Going from irony which is too sarcastic to humor which is at the same time humility and amity. Renouncing asperity. Preferring Yes to

No. And how many shades of meaning in the contrast that was once so rigidly erected between religion and faith! "After all, one can only see one side of the moon at a time."

However, there are justifiable angers such as those expressed openly by the prophets. The luxury of Bethel, fruit of injustice, aroused the indignation of Amos. The lazy complicity of the priest serving at the local sanctuary, his complaint to the king, the threats of exile, did not prevent the man of God from saying what he had to say. He was violent; but in a holy way. Anger is too often cheapened by wounded self-love, personal claims, and an obsessive preoccupation with the self. Anger can be a virtue; it can also recoil on itself as a hidden selfishness and become a show. The misery of men is a scandal for anyone endowed with sensitivity; but I do not think that it can be answered with another scandal: that of an anger unpurified by prayer. And even when our blood seethes because of sins among churchmen such as compromises with conscience, silence, lies. . . . There is no such thing as a spectacular achievement of maturity. Neither can there be one without courage.

It is difficult to talk seriously about God. Yet, we must do it. Am I not under the obligation to talk seriously about God to myself? Talking to God implies talking about God, even in the privacy of the self. Otherwise, I run the risk of slipping unconsciously into the adoration of a hybrid divinity, a bit pagan, a bit Jewish, a bit Christian. As a priest I do not want to withhold from my brothers this talk to God and about God which is the root of my consecrated life. Should it happen that, having to talk about God, I wish to touch upon other matters—changing the world, social justice, economical or political revolution—I must first make sure that I am not escaping from my own depth. The depth of the others can only be reached through one's own depth. If I am tempted to cease talking about God to others, it may be that I have stopped talking about him to myself. It may also be that language has become a barrier between others and myself. I live off God but, dependent upon worn-out concepts that I am unable in my clumsiness to clothe in vigor and taste, I am aware that what is for me (beneath the words or even without words) wealth and youthfulness, reaches the ears of my listeners—even the alert ones—as a fossilized discourse.

How bitter it can be: not to be able to talk to others about God when I never cease to talk about him to myself! But the strongest temptation presents itself when I think that I can perceive almost nowhere in my environment the least bit of attention to God, of interest in him. The conditions of life are a hinderance. Violence instigated or suffered under the most variegated disguises. The mechanization of everything. Slavery to usefulness. Overwhelming concerns. In such a world there is no room for gratuitousness. It is then that, giving up the talk about God, countering deafness with dumbness, many want to devote themselves to changing life.

One must indeed change life, but this does not mean that one should give up talking about God. To change life as best as possible. To talk about God in the least harmful way. All becomes confused when one gives in to the perennial temptation of politics first, of which Maurras held the monopoly only for a while. Taking this formula literally would mean to accept its corollary: never to talk about God. Now, people are too quick to conclude peremptorily that the men of our time are deaf. They are always a bit hard of hearing; they are never totally deaf. Misunderstandings are numerous. They can even be tragic. But dehumanization is only a limit: as long as man is man, he is so by God's desire. Such, at least, is my faith. I do not want to run the risk of being dumber than men are deaf.

A future complete change of life is even more totally a delusion than the one Rimbaud had—with a mixture of enchantment and hesitation—when he asked himself in his delirium of the Infernal Husband: How many hours did I stay awake at night, wondering why he wanted so much to escape reality? He may have the formula for *changing life*? No, he is only looking for it, I told myself. Modern utopia has transposed the words that the poet had stressed, putting them in the language of political and social action, at times neglecting to strip them of their poetic and magic power which is valid in its own order but only in such an order. To transform society is hard work, most often obscure work shared by all and coexistent with the history of mankind. It belongs neither to a specific time nor a specific place. No one has been exempted from participation in the genesis of man. A poet plays the part for which he was elected. He is irreplaceable because he intuits and forebodes gratuitousness as the ultimate vocation. Though in a deeper sense all men are elected. Chosen by the grace of God to labor so that man may become more human.

A mystical error has been made: despising that which is temporal. There are one hundred terrible pages in *Véronique* accusing the clerics of having "given birth to the disaster of a totally dechristianized world." But Péguy is right in saying that this was a "mystical error," not a tactical one. I do not wish to imply that the Church is becoming a tactician today and acts for its own interests, with the afterthought of winning people back into the fold when it reminds men of their duties as men. I am careful not to fall into overkill. Neither do I want anybody to think that Christian faith can become the Ariadne thread for those who attempt to do away with inequalities and injustices and find themselves in the maze of economical and political mediations. To search for techniques and implement them is a matter of conscience, intelligence and courage.

But there is Another present in my freedom. The one who talks to me, to whom I talk, and of whom I talk. He is in me more myself than I am; therefore he is not exterior to my reasons for acting. His presence is Word and Act. He tells me that I am in the world in order to love as he loves; he makes me capable of so loving. This gift is called by the Church: the grace of God. God is pure gratuitousness: he imparts to me his Being of gratuitousness. In him, there is no shade of calculation: he offers to me—this is the meaning of creative initiative—to participate in his Life, without any calculation. At this peak of himself, man is man. I cannot accept to see him wanting to be less. Were I to become flexible on this point, I would deny my faith or would be mistaken about its substance. By the same token, I would sooner or later become vulnerable to the many-faceted objection of unbelief. To have a specifically Christian motivation in temporal commitment is to enable all men to have access to this free recognition of love's absolute gratuitousness. It would be impossible to avoid the maze of complex mediations in which justice is a matter of priority. But such a complexity will not make me give up the simplicity of the ultimate end, and the latter gives its deepest meaning to the present.

Emmanuel Mounier said: "The fact that those who hold eternity have lost the meaning of the temporal order should not make us lose the sense of eternity in the grasp we have regained on temporal reality." We used to plead with the national Chaplaincy of Youth Organizations to stop the long-standing policy of systematic ignorance of the specifically political dimension of problems. However, we were not tempted to shrink faith to such a dimension. We used to say, in the style of the time: "Extension in the temporal order, concentration in the spiritual order." The young men and young girls were suspicious of chatty and shallow theologies in which, as Mounier said, divine matters are "manhandled with a nauseating tactlessness." Things have not changed today. I am sure that people would eagerly welcome a theological and pastoral approach endowed with a sober and vigorous character, taking seriously the mystery of man and the mystery of God and in which there would be no trace of contempt for the people. Amid many words that quickly became slogans and are already on their way out such as *to adapt, to liberate, to destructure,* I would like to see other words such as *to deepen, to interiorize, to discern.*

Marcel Maréchal, who was the director of an avant-garde theater and an agnostic to boot, was asked what he thought about the "questioning" in the Church. He replied: "If it is taking place because the priests of the Catholic religion want to go ahead in the world so that Catholicism might become more Christian, meaning closer to a true social action . . . if this great movement is a progressive movement, if it aims to make the Church more humanistic, it does not seem important to me, it even seems disappointing. If it is on the contrary, a great movement meant to give back to the Church its true function, namely to give priority to the people who see, to the mystics, then it appears to me as more interesting and more important. Taking off one's cassock or getting married will not solve the problems of faith. If this is a forward leap, if the priest gets rid of his chores in the young men's club, Catholic action, etc., to tell himsef 'I am a man of God, I must only witness to my faith and to God,' then I am interested. In other words, if this is a mystical adventure, I find it fascinating. If it is a social adventure in the fashion of our time, if the pastors are suddenly touched by socialist grace, I am only bored; I think that it is regressive."[1] It is a shame that Marcel Maréchal does not seem to have understood why, and precisely because theirs is a mystical adventure, priests must lean towards those who are rejected by society. Moreover, his thought is hazy, his vocabulary ill-defined and his angle too narrow. But the arrow is sharp.

Gratuitousness is perhaps the least inadequate word if we want to express the mystery of man and the mystery of God. It includes in its meaning purity of love, freedom, absence of calculation. Grace and gratitude have the same root. Grace is gratuitousness, gratitude is a response of gratuitousness and homage. In this world of utility and necessity, there is a need for a pedagogy of gratuitousness. If there is a meaning to the expression political theology, this is where we must seek it. I know masters of literature, and even of science who are also masters of gratuitousness. The word is neither technical nor pedantic. Yet one must beware of its possible reminder of André Gide: Lafcadio was not on God's way. However, everyone knows that a gesture has something disinterested or useless. The gratuitousness of Bach or Mozart—a desire which is not a need, mingled with joy, hope and contrition—could be felt by teenagers, at least if they were taught through experience, even through childish experience.

But a teacher leads to gratuitousness only if he feeds upon it. Art is an initiation. I believe that I would never have dared talk about God if I had not prayed to him at length on the notes of the Gregorian Gradual. It was this sublime chant that taught me to deny, in one sweeping move of the soul, both the dryness of rationalism and the falsehood of sentimentality. To give in to one or the other of these attitudes means to destroy the true image of God which lives inside ourself. He ceases to be a beating heart. One must use words. But let them reach the ears of others, fresh and as it were still covered with the dew that brought them forth! Blessed is timidity—which has nothing to do with doctrinal hesitation—when one becomes aware that the inner music of the word is so rich, so intimate and so pure, that it is hardly possible to utter such a word, even if one were a Monk of Solesmes, without somehow degrading it a little. As in *l'Annonce faite à Marie* (The Annunciation to Mary, by Paul Claudel), where maidenly modesty reflects the same feeling.

This modesty is at the same time a reserve and an emotion. Let us read Rimbaud: "In the wood, there is a bird, its song will make you stop and blush." And Gregory Nazianzen: "This shiver in my voice, my spirit and my thought which I sense each time I talk about God, wishing you the same laudable and blessed feeling." How much more then, if one believes that the Depth of the Deity, as Meister Eckhart says, is this Power of self-effacement that theology, following Saint Paul, calls *kenosis*! It is impossible to talk about the *kenosis* of God unless one does it, as it were, kenotically. To suggest the humility of God, can only be done in humility. Kenotic voice: not one who has given up speech, but one who disappears within the word itself.

"Beloved," said Saint Leo, "the greatness of the divine work is far beyond the power of human language; hence it is difficult to talk while one has a reason not to be silent (*difficultas fandi, ratio non tacendi*). . . . Let us then rejoice in our powerlessness to talk about such a great mercy, and since we cannot express the sublimity of the mystery of our salvation, let us feel how good for us it is to be thus defeated. For no one can come closer to the knowledge of truth than he who understands that in the matter of divine mysteries, he will always have much to seek, even if he has already advanced very far. He who presumes having already attained what he is seeking, does not find what he is looking for, but is failing in his quest."[2]

Silence is not dumbness. Dumbness is a vacuum of words born of the vacuum of the soul. But silence nourishes the soul. Before even starting to praise those whose task it is to talk about God, I will indulge in a long digression on Claudel: "In Claudel," says Charles du Bos, "as in all the greatest geniuses, the voice is all. It is the voice of a man who, even though he is not conscious of this, hardly dares *talk to himself* . . . the hum of an almost uninterrupted intimate psalmody is heard throughout his life: he talks to himself, and suddenly he *talks*, and the first word is never the first one: there are behind it and in it all these hums that had never been voiced, it is the emerging peak of a whole sum of whispers that had been hidden until then and for quite a long time. The first word of Claudel is the slow emergence of a net carrying all its load; the load is heavy and tends to drag the net back. This is what lends to the thrust of *La Messe là-bas* (The Mass Down There) its submarine quality, its nostalgia, and its prestige."[3]

But beyond this humming psalmody which is already the expression of a self-recollected soul, there is the more fundamental unity of poetry and music. Such a unity lies in the most intimate part of the being. It lies, to use the words of Jean Cassou, "lower than the probe could reach." It is not yet poetry or music, it is Silence, an abyss of silence (*Sigè l'Abîme* [dormant abyss] is the concluding expression of *Connaissance du temps* [*Knowledge of the Time*]). Saint Augustine and the most metaphysical among mystics have used the word Memory to describe this zone of solitude which precedes the operations of the faculties, which is even anterior to their distinction, anterior therefore *a fortiori* to the techniques of art. It is there that man escapes from time through his own summit. It would be useless to attempt a quest on the psychological or historical level of *Animus*, if we did not at first reside in the secret kingdom of *Anima*, where "in the silence of silence Mnemosyne is sighing." In truth, all starts with the Muse of Memory who is indivisibly the memory of self and the memory of God. To quote the magnificent text of the First Ode:

> "The eldest, the one who talks not!
> The eldest,whose age is the same!
> Mnemosyne who never talks!
> She listens, she considers.
> She feels (being inner sense of the spirit),
> Pure, simple, inviolable! She remembers.
> She is spiritual weight.
> She is the ratio expressed by a very beautiful cipher.
> She stands in an ineffable manner

On the very pulse of the Being.
She is the inner hour; the treasure that
springs forth and the source that is contained;
The junction to what is not time of the
time expressed by language.
She will not talk; she is intent on not talking.
She coincides. She possesses, she remembers,
and all her sisters are intently
watching the flutter of her eyelids."

In a later work, Claudel evoked a music "so beautiful that (he) could only prefer silence to it." Silence, source and purpose of art. Silence at the beginning and silence at the end. One must 'sow' it in the hearts of men. This is the task of the artist, unless he gives in to the pleasure of aesthetic juggling, of sloppy calisthenics. If silence is solitude, it is also communion. Which is why the absolute beyond of expression may only be a limitation. Mnemosyne is not Eternity, but a junction of eternity and time. Therefore, she is not alone, and all her sisters, the Muses, are intently watching the flutter of her eyelids. Silence is then already music. It is already a note. At first a lone note, at the border between music and silence. Mallarmé had described a female saint on a stained glass window as a "musician of silence." Claudel himself said that the musician Muse, Euterpe, "holy flamina of the spirit," holds in her hands "the great insonorous lyre." Insonorous, yet sonorous. "I hear the sole note blossom with an invincible eloquence." Euterpe is not the one who sings, she is song itself in the moment of its creation . . . invention of the marvelous question, clear dialog with inexhaustible silence.

"Inexhaustible" is the pre-eminent attribute of mystery. Claudel contrasts it with "countable." The clear dialog expresses in poetry the infinite riches of the primordial Silence while awaiting the final, eternal Silence of Beatitude. In *Le Soulier de satin* (The Satin Slipper), a woman is called Music. Doña Music or Doña Delight. She holds a guitar but never plays it. In the heart of drama now extended to the measure of the Universe, she is also the musician of silence. But after twenty-five years of meditation on the Bible and the Fathers of the Church, the universe of the poet became charged with symbols. The woman is at the center, symbolizing the human soul and the Church, the deepest interiority and the most universal communion. Agitation and noise are a hindrance to them. In order for men to be able to see one another and to discover how unique each face is, they first must keep silent and listen to the Music who does not play her guitar. "Do you then believe," the young man tells the young girl, "that joy is a thing to be given and to be received such as it is? The joy that you give me, you will see it on the face of the others." And in the great baroque church of Saint Nicholas in Prague, Music thanks God for being music:

> It is enough for a little soul to be simple enough and start and then all the others, even without wanting to do so, start to listen and respond, and they agree. Beyond the borders, we will establish this enchanted republic where souls visit one another on skiffs that are so tiny that one tear is enough to ballast them. We are not the ones who make music, she is here, nothing can escape her, we only have to adapt ourselves, to sink into music up to our ears and beyond. Rather than opposing things, we only have to deftly sail on their blessed motion.

From silence to language, from language to silence: such is the motion of life lived as poetry. It is the motion of any life that is not shocked by games. When the language of God is not perceived as having been born out of silence, and remaining immersed in it all along its course, no one will listen. Perhaps the only listener would be a conservative who hates novelty. How mediocre is a repetitive language! Neglecting distinctions and nuances, students translate: magisterial course. The Gospel called this: word of the scribes. The people listened to Jesus because he did not talk "like the scribes" (Mk 1:22).

Elijah at Horeb heard the coming of God. Neither in the wind, nor in the earthquake, nor in the fire but "in the sound of a gentle breeze" (1 K 19:11-13) which Emmanuel Lévinas translates as "the voice of a fine silence."[4] And Olivier Clément calls it: "A word at the end of silence."[5] To each his own experience and his way of overcoming, in expressing it, the mockery of the words. Once, during a very quiet night, I heard the light kiss of the softest rain on the tenderest grass: God was there. Quoting Claudel again, when his Angel instructs Prouhèze:

> . . . . If someone is all caught up and prisoner of the conversation, if he hears a violin playing somewhere, or simply two or three successive taps on a piece of wood, little by little, he will become silent, he has been interrupted, he is elsewhere as the saying goes, he lends an ear.
>
> And what about you? Tell me whether it is true that you have never heard in the depths of yourself, between heart and liver, this dull knock, this peremptory stop, this urgent touch?

Delusion? Perhaps. Is this really God who is passing? Who can guarantee that it is not myself talking to myself, or enchanting myself with a dream? The poet is self-confident, but the mocking psychologist smiles. We live in a time of "reducers." Thus it is impossible to bypass laborious reflections. One must go on to philosophy. But no analytical or critical process has the power to engender its own origin. One searches and finds only that which is already there. To forget this would be usurping the name of "metaphysics" and all would wind up in abstraction. This is how ideologies multiply.

From a Christ without God to a God without Christ, I can

see my contemporaries wavering. Jesuism or deism: more than one is viewing this as a simplified proposition. A Christ without God—horizontal, as the lingo would have it—is this superior, exceptional, undoubtedly unique in history, perhaps even superhuman, man who has been able to reveal mankind to itself. He has opened for humanity the roads to freedom. At the most, he frees us from the most oppressive and jealous authority: that of Almighty God. Being an incomparable model of altruism, he is at the same time and indivisibly the one who reveals the life of man and the death of God. Such would be the Good News. There is no call to deride this, unless one were to systematically ignore the complexity of background hidden under an abrupt and overstated language. We shall oppose to this "Christian" theology of the death of God in Jesus Christ—which will like all excesses bordering on absurdity, be soon forgotten—the revelation in Jesus Christ of the humility of God.

A God without Christ, is the God of philosophers and scientists. The Absolute of whom one could not believe that he took flesh while remaining the Absolute. The Truth that can only cease to be universal if it encloses itself within the particularity of a historically determined individual. Such a wavering is not especially new, although more people are affected and troubled by it nowadays. For those who profess a belief in the divinity of Jesus Christ, the danger seems to lean towards a poorly disguised fideism. If it's permitted to judge as excessive the opposition Pascal once described between the God of the philosophers and of the scientists and the God of Abraham, Isaac and Jacob, how much more abusive then is the manner with which it is too frequently used today in a pastoral language fearful, above all, of the least sliding into abstract intellectualism! It remains true that the slope is dangerous on this side too. People gave in to it for too long a time. Today, the anti-intellectual drive is stronger. One lets oneself be carried away to the very edge of a faith which cannot be declared pure unless it is not justified at all by reason. As if the act of believing did not have, more than any other, to be founded on something! If it is not founded, it remains at the level of a feeling or is volatilized away when the most elementary psychological analysis proves it to be delusory. Then one finds out that it is quite possible to do without Jesus Christ just as atheists do without God.

Alternate unilateralisms, which are a constant trait of history, reach to the borders of excess during periods of crisis. The latent conflict that begets them is between the head and the heart, reason and feeling. Such an opposition is really a superficial one for, as Péguy said: "There is a pathetic side of thought while there is a light and clarity of heart. There is even a pathetic side to reason. There is a pathetic climate of thought and there is a climate of knowledge of the heart."[6] One should therefore not cast aspersions on reason or feeling. But there are ambiguities here and there, and they must be cleared away, otherwise one will not be able to understand that in the quest for God, living experience and logical discourse must be closely embraced to each other.

Reason itself, in its concrete use, can be called feeling. When it is so understood, it belongs to the order of knowledge and not that of sensitivity. It is knowledge itself as a "realization" of an idea, as Newman would have said. It can also be called its interiorization, so that in the end it becomes myself. It is then that it becomes power and life. And one can talk about "taste." Sapientia and sapor have the same root. The being is not tasteless. If mystics have a taste for God, it means that God has a taste. The word is no more daring than many others.

Sensitivity, though distinct from this knowledge, is not alien to it. Of course, this does not concern what people call emotivity or mawkishness, most often a matter for the nerves finding an outlet in easy tears. We are talking about love as a natural thing. The proof of its genuine character is that it cares nothing for intruding frequently into consciousness through sensible manifestations. When it does become conscious, all of myself emerges from the depths. And beyond, it translates itself in a warm devotion in action, an intuitive finesse of feelings, an inventive spontaneity. The heart. A man of heart. Cordiality means at the same time strength and simplicity. Concrete knowledge and controlled sensitivity meet at this central point—my most intimate self—where intelligence and will are united before they branch off. There, already, we find a carnal, a visceral harmony. Because man is one.

I cannot let it be said that God cannot be an object of proof. Yet I know that today the word seems suspicious to many people, and it is not merely a matter of fashion. The present decline of rational arguments in pastoral guidance is not a sudden appearance of irrationality sought for its own sake. When I take its causes seriously, I am aware that I cannot anymore let it be said purely and simply that God is an object of proof. God, an object? One should say: necessarily and unduly objectivated. Necessarily, otherwise I would have to keep silent. Unduly, because God is not an object among others, even if he were the first one, credited afterward with a transcendental meaning. He is the Absolute, and the Absolute is not relative to anything or to anyone. To be precise, one should not call him transcendent, because the verb "to transcend" is not intransitive: the act of transcending calls for an object, implies a relation. Any discursive reasoning entails an elaboration of relations, to be as precise as possible, which circumscribe the object under study and distinguish it from all that is not itself.

No such thing is possible when one talks about God. Therefore intelligence must not become a dupe of its own operation and has to exert its autocritical faculties. On the other hand, one cannot look for God without starting from God. If he is reached at the end of a logical process, it is because he was present at the start. Present, though not recognized. He is the one through whom I exist as a thinking being. It is his act that makes a spirit of me, now. God is God only if he is the one outside of whom there is nothing. Otherwise, whatever I discover in my reasonings is not him. God is proved only by recognizing him. Any rational knowledge of God is a recognition. Thus, when a beam of sparkling rays breaks through a leaden sky, I realize that all I had seen before I saw the sun, was made visible to me through its light. A day without sunshine is day only because of the sun itself. If, at the end of the way I affirm the absolute, this affirmation can only be silence. In fact, nothing could be said but in terms of relation, which would be a contradiction to my affirmation of Being without relation. Unless . . . , since he initiated the process that has been completed, another initiative uttered as explicit Word enables me to go yet further and to talk, in my turn, in terms of an explicitly confessed faith.

I shall therefore persist in talking about God. But my thought will be directed in a simple way, without parting from experience which stands at its starting point. Simplicity, refusal to break away from living reality: these two conditions are essential for the proof to be human, I would even dare say popular in the real meaning of the word, which is noble and robust. Simplicity is not over-simplification. Those who are the most tempted by over-simplification are people who have a little bit of science or even a great deal of it, and who tend to approach the question of the ultimate meaning of existence as if it were one of the questions of mathematics or physics. To prove or demonstrate cannot mean the same thing here and there. What should already make us wary is the fact that mathematics is not subject to the same type of proofs as physics. In the former, one has to deduce and in the latter, to experiment; there one infers, here one formulates a law.

It is thus enough to have some familiarity with scientific

methods in order to accept the fact that each discipline has original proofs, proper to itself. And to accept at the same time—questioning about the absolute belonging to a completely different order—that the proof being sought will be structured in a totally different way. In the sciences, a particular coherence or system of coherence is to be brought to light. When we come to God, we are dealing with the Universal, Reality itself. It is not possible to transfer to the field of freedom the very type of proof which is valid in the world of necessity. Yet in our time technique is the rule, and the road to simplicity is obstructed. Being used to look for the *how* of things, the mind has lost the habit of naively asking *why?* We must go back to a certain candor. It must be an alert candor, though. Experience does not necessarily imply a consciousness of experience. Most of the time, we live without looking at ourselves in the process of living. Some circumstances do call for attention. When Claudel wrote some pages about the paralytic people of Berck, he entitled his work *"Les invités à l'attention"* (*Invited to attention*). He addresses them:

"You envy all those people who stand, move and act, but are you sure that they are as alive as you are? Could it be that life is no more for them than a dream in which the round of ideas and acts, habits and gestures, operates as it were, by itself and almost without any thought? To you, God gave a bitter leisure. Is not the taste of a bunch of cherries, for instance, quite different for a sated diner who pecks at them absentmindedly at the end of a good meal than it is for a thirsty and hungry traveler who savors them not only with his mouth and palate, but from the depths of his heart and his stomach? Does not a bunch of beautiful fresh flowers, or a plate overflowing with heavy clusters of grapes, bring more joy to the bedside of a sick man than to the table of a Parisian lady sitting down to tea? On the one hand, eye and mind barely touch the matter: the slave cannot stop for a second, he has to go on to his tasks. On the other hand, there is a communion, and the solemn presence of all these God-made beautiful things takes on something of a sacramental nature. . . ."[7]

No one is compelled to give attention to life in its vitality. We are only invited. Such an attention is free. How much more then is attention to the fundamental question: what is the meaning of this bubbling, radiant or crushing life? Where does it come from and where does it go? Why is it? No man can totally avoid such a question, unless he has ceased to be man. But the attention can become a prisoner, wrapped up in this "inexhaustible stream of beautiful appearances" of which Proust wrote. It needs a quiet place in order to focus. Otherwise "eye and mind barely touch the matter." Here freedom prevails. The question is compelling, but we are not compelled to give our attention to the question. Many are those who call it irrelevant, more useless than these "appearances," even though they are recognized as such, but are so beautiful even when they hurt, that people choose to prefer them. Then the questioning about the meaning of existence becomes blurred and finally vanishes. It comes to the point, as Gide put it, of no-need-is-felt-anymore.

A free act is thus the origin of the proof of God. One must stress this because nowhere on our road to it will we find an argument that compels the mind. Freedom stands at the start, and it is also at the end, therefore along the way. But where there is freedom, there is also reason. If man is free it is because he is rational. As I recognize freedom on the threshold of my venture, I also must find reason there. Hence one must guard against opposing experience and rationality. Rationality is present in the most humble experience of man, otherwise it would not be the experience of a man, but of an animal. Intellection is often confused with abstraction. Not without cause: intelligence is always tempted to turn into a game of concepts that can enchant it without realizing that the tie with reality has been broken. It is experience that is real. Outside of it, the necessary conceptualization—how could one think without concepts?—destroys the mind, impells it to move in the delusion of systems. Péguy is one of those who saw the danger with the greatest eloquence, indignation and humor:

"Today, all the texts are vanishing under commentaries, all the living texts are lying dead under the mute dust and under the chatter of marginal notes, all minds are frozen under letters, all people are sunk in demography, societies under sociology, monuments fallen under archeology, inscriptions shattered under epigraphy, the frescoes are peeling, nations disappear under demagogy, childhood itself disappears under pedagogy, all life vanishes under the shroud of census, invention is dead, instinct is petrified in intellect . . . race, sap, source, all is buried under this funeral trail, this snowy, spongy, filthy trail of ashes."[8]

One does not go from ashes to God. But living experience without reason is also ashes, in its own way. To attend to interrogation about the meaning of life, which is an act of freedom and of reason, is also an act of faith. There is a *yes to meaning*, outside of which the question itself has no meaning. This does not mean that I prejudge the answer or that I enclose it unduly within the terms of the question: that would be begging the question. But there is in man a daring to exist which is as fundamental as existence itself. The two are consubstantial. Spinoza called this daring *conatus*, Nabert: *original affirmation*, and Blondel: *action*. Without such a hope (of which it can be said—and the meanings are equivalent—that it is natural or that it is the first act of freedom) no failure would be felt as failure or disappointment. Kant deems faith in meaning to be rational. I can deny it or pretend to deny it but then, to use the words of Father Auguste Valentin, all that is left to me is to get out of the being by slamming the doors.

To cease wavering between feeling and abstraction, to

keep rationality and living experience held by a tight knot, to accept that logical discourse can be rerouted on the condition that it emerges from silence and can return to silence, to be on guard against any form of philosophical "neurasthenia," and to trust in the humble reason that makes man man: such are the conditions which can be proposed as some preparations for a rational affirmation of God.[9] Immediate experience is both an experience of meaning and of absurdity. There is a meaning. The positive sciences discover in the world of nature structures, coherences, laws: a meaning is included there. Historical endeavor toward a society that is more just, more brotherly, more one in its diversity, has *a* meaning. Human relations—companionship, friendship, love—have *a* meaning. Art—Bach, Mozart, Rembrandt—has *a* meaning. *A certain meaning*. At this initial point of our study, it does not matter that Claude Lévi-Strauss, for one, suspects that this meaning, such as it is generally lived and recognized, is not the real one, and wants to find it in infrastructures which are not grasped by spontaneous consciousness and direct observation. I say simply, elementarily, and naively: there is *a* meaning. This is unimpeachable.

There is also *an* absurdity. Here is a splendid young girl lying on a hospital bed who weeps and tells me that a cancer is devouring her. I can only be as revolted as she is, faced with absurdity. The tidal wave that causes thousands of men to starve is absurdity. Absurd too is the hell of Sartre in which people cannot live together though they can neither cease to live together. Absurd above all, is the betrayal that destroys for an abandoned woman or man, all purpose of existence. Absurdity is no less unimpeachable than meaning. Meaning and absurdity are mingled as the wheat and the weeds of the parable. But absurdity is stronger than meaning, even the most joyful and magnificent meaning. For on the one hand, it latches on to it and corrodes it: the particular being is precarious and in motion towards its death. "All goes underground and is absorbed into the game," as Valéry dares to say. For liberty, which has emerged from nature, to be defeated by it, this is absurdity in itself.

On the other hand, particular meanings, indefinitely accumulated do not amount to a global meaning. There is no immediate universal meaning. All is *here*, no more. Hence the fundamental question of Heidegger: "Why is there something and not nothing?" In a more radical way yet, since the questioner cannot exclude himself from the question: Why am I here, asking why? The particular meanings are powerless to lend a meaning to everything: if everything had meaning, I would not ask: why? But this immediate absurdity of everything does affect the particular meanings, so that from the very heart of science, art, friendship, love, historical endeavor—in short, life itself—the "why?" is born and reborn ceaselessly. This is the trial that the philosophers call contingency. This is a trial in the two meanings of the word: experience and suffering. A reflected experience, therefore a human one. Suffering, because the questioner shivers under the touch of the wind of absurdity. He breaks loose from himself, as Claudel puts it in the technical language of the watchmakers. If there were no meaning anywhere, one would have to, in spite of being dizzy, accept the absurdity of all and everything.

But meaning is unimpeachable. Existence is therefore not absurd: it is contradictory. I could stop right here. No one is constraining me. But then I would just have to keep silent. Because if I refuse to overcome contradiction, thus cancelling the question about man, it is man himself in his rationality that I destroy. I cannot consent to this. Which is why I affirm the absolute, "source of all meanings, and foundation, the presence of which is rightly felt and deeply so in the conjunction of the meanings, though they remain truly particular, and of the contingency which is immediately absurd." (E. Pousset). In other words, to admit contingency and to recognize the absolute amounts to one same and indivisible act of reason and freedom.

There is nothing scientific in this proof. No compelling argument. Therefore, I would not be surprised by the reproaches of projection and alienation that people will not fail to hurl at me. It would be naive not to expect them. In fact, it is only the humility of God—which is for me the deepest secret of his mystery—that convinces me of their being ridiculous. However, at this stage of the way, I can already challenge them, on the grounds of a moral and intellectual demand. Indeed, I do not affirm the absolute as correlative with contingency. How could I? If contingency were tied to the absolute by a necessary bond, it would cease being contingency. I would destroy it in the very act by which I test it. Or, to put it in another way, Necessity would cancel it by establishing it.

The contingent being is therefore related to the absolute only if the absolute is non-relation towards contingency. God is not for the world. God is not for me. He is. I can affirm him only by dispossessing myself. Gratuitousness is already here, to be carried to its highest degree by faith. I will have to remember this, lest the God of Abraham, Isaac and Jacob be adored with less gratuitousness and because of his promises, than the God of no promises described by the philosophers and the scientists. The danger is not a chimera, as I know only too well! However, grace would not be grace if it were not the offer to go beyond in gratuitousness.

This absolute that I affirm, I can and I must call useless. Even later on, I may say that it is the useless that is the most useful! But then the word takes on a new meaning: it refers to the highest level of existence—the existence outside of self—which man is thus given to hope for. By pointing to the presence of the absolute in the heart of contingency—nocturn presence, presence in the mode of absence—I already commit myself to want for himself the One who is valid in himself, to recognize God as God. The rational and free recognition of God commits to a moral obligation.

Being such as I am, I cannot believe that a commitment in faith—philosophical faith and religious faith—to the useless could be a delusory projection. And even less an immoral alienation. And yet! People tell me sometimes with such emphasis that, as a believer, I lack courage when faced with reality, that I am troubled now and then. Be that as it may, it is not difficult for me, confronted with the boundless Majesty of the useless, to realize that even though my faith can at times appear as cowardice in my own eyes, it is precisely then that my God has ceased being the God who is.

If God were useless, would not common sense invite us to deny him? I hear whispers: What do we need this luxury for? Indeed, common sense . . . that of Satan in the desert of Judea, or that of Herod sending Jesus back to Pilate. For either one, master and minion, experts in common sense, Jesus is useless. My job, as a priest, is to break the circle of usefulness and to carry on patiently, however difficult the task may be, the education to gratuitousness. To affirm God because he is useful, to deny him because he is useless: two opposite sides of the same mediocrity. When luxury seems nonessential to man, it is because man barely started to be man, or is skidding on the slope where he will cease to be man.

The common experience of strangeness points to a road that can lead to the verge of pure adoration. It is possible, starting with the other relatively other whom we see, to intuit the Other absolutely other whom we do not see amd whom we call God. To be a stranger is to be torn away from the security of familiar things: environment, horizon, framework of life, ideas, opinions, tastes. If we are familiar with classical music, we feel strange when confronted with the techniques of Boulez and Xenakis. We were born in Bach's land: we have to change countries, to cross a border beyond which another language is spoken. Nostalgia for the "already heard" and the "well known" prevents us from giving in to the attraction of novelty, and we tremble in its presence. The home of Bach was our home. To leave it is to leave our own home. Aesthetic exodus is a dispossession.

So is any exodus. But earthly exodus is only half an exodus. The other, up to a certain point, is still the same. In the sun flooding the piles of golden fruit on the Arab markets, I recognize my pale French sun. No mutation of culture or civilization is deep enough for me not to discern some elements of my near or distant past. And to see our human brothers as others, without treating them as mere satellites of ourselves is an effort of charity, the success of which is the only limit. But God! He is not the same in anything. Not only Other, not only All-Other, but as Abbé Monchanin used to say: All-Otherly other. Which permits us to say that he is Non-Other. Concepts and words, wrought for the expression of Sameness, can only burst apart. Mystics wear themselves out to invent a vocabulary which denies what they affirm and affirms what they deny. They say: Superdeity, Superessence, Nothingness, Supernothingness. But they are not deceived. They know that all these expressions are failing. Blondel points out that the words "divine nature," found in the second epistle of Peter—*divinae consortes naturae*—are themselves failing because, as he says: "One could not reflect too much about this: God has no nature, he was not born (*natura* was derived from *nascor*); he can therefore not be assimilated to that which is subject to or receives from what does not come from himself alone: *ratio sui est*."[10]

Since one must talk, and talk simply, I say along with a tradition that is more common than the mystical one: God is mystery. But then I must be careful not to use this word in order to describe that part of the unknown, which in spite of the progress of the sciences, remains in nature and might perhaps always remain in it. I must also guard against restricting its meaning by giving it only the content of what goes beyond our spontaneous imagery of the divine: it would be yet another way of "locating" God with regard to the human mind, thus relativizing him. Mystery is the infinite of the Ineffable. In Heaven, says Saint John of the Cross, "the elect who know God the best understand the most distinctly the infinitude that they still have to understand."[11] Such is the fullness of joy: not to reach the end of the "counting" but to grasp the "inexhaustible" such as it is. Not to understand but to welcome without mediation and in love that which cannot be understood.

Mystery recognized at last as Mystery in itself. It would not be by biting on mystery that man could accomplish himself, in the fashion of a scientist who bites on an unknown factor of nature and tears off a piece of being out of the night of a temporary irrationality. Mystery is not a temporary mystery. The Other is Other forever. If he were to cease being so, how could one love him absolutely? There is no love without recognition of an otherness. Love is absolute, and is love of the Absolute, only in the absolute recognition of the absolute Otherness. Eternal life is not an absorption into God: to identify with Mystery would be a negation of Mystery. This was well understood by these "mystics of will" who were less highly speculative than the "mystics of intelligence," but undoubtedly humbler, and thus deeper. I am thinking about Saint Bernard, Saint Francis de Sales, Fénelon. They all tell us that union with God and distinction from Him do not grow in inverse proportion, but in equal proportion. The perfection of the one is the perfection of the other.

I dare not say that religion starts where philosophy ends. It would be a highly rigid and superficial interpretation of Blondel's dialectics—and perhaps already those of Pascal—to imagine faith picking up after reason, when the latter having become exhausted by its last efforts, leaves the problems of man without solutions. Nothing is feigned in *L'Action*: Blondel is both a philosopher and a Christian. When he undertakes to show that an ultimate demand is necessarily implied in each human volition, he certainly imposes upon himself a restriction to the sole resources of reflective thought. It can thus be said that he speaks *as* a philosopher. But the "as" is not devoid of ambiguity, whether he be the philosopher, the exegete or the scientist. One could not deny that a discipline has specific methods and that confusion, no matter in what field, should be avoided at all cost. However, there cannot be an absolute separation between a method and the man who implements it. A specialist always locates his specialty within his full humanity. Any particular approach supposes a totality which is globally comprehended from the start. Of course, this brings up a delicate matter of honesty that no one could solve *a priori*.

Deism, which was triumphant in the XVIIIth century, managed to disintegrate the totality of faith. It is powerless to restore it. If a living being is cut up, one should know that it cannot be reconstituted, unless by some artifice. I would be quite clumsy if I were to give here the impression that I want to go from deism to faith, giving the floor to myself *before* letting God talk, establishing the rationality of affirming God *before* hearing him tell me who he is. There is no *before*. There is a *within*: it is from within the Revelation comprehended in its integrality that I invite my reason to listen to the word of the Ineffable. To listen, when it comes to reason, means to want to understand. The rational confession of the existence of God is immanent to faith.

The One of whom one cannot talk, talks. The Ineffable manifests and expresses himself. On what grounds would my reason forbid him to do so? Or how can one deny freedom to the Infinite? Will it be said that there is a contradiction in affirming at the same time that God is the Being without relation and that he decides to enter into a relation? Such a question implies a presupposition: that of a monolithic God who would be somehow compelled to be only what he is. The contradiction is rather to be found in imagining that infinite freedom could be prey to some necessity. Moreover, could one conceive a God who would not be love? Revelation tells us to what extent love can go, to what unheard-of degree of gratuitousness it can reach: the death of Christ, the offer of a share in divine life to the creature. But when this generosity is unveiled to us, it reaches a secret part of our being that was waiting for it since God had impressed such a desire when he impressed his image in us.

If man is not alert to his own mystery, his talk about God becomes an empty logomachy. Yet, respect is due to those who have a passion for humanity but fail to call "God" the "divine" aspect they perceive in men. Saint-John Perse tells us that the poet whose function is "the very deepening of the mystery of man," when he has dived into this "expanding universe" which is "the moral infinity" of a soul, comes up to the surface "charged with a brief phosphorescence." He has seen that "the divine spark forever lives in the human flint." He can then praise "the pride of man marching under his load of eternity." "Assisted only by the flashes of intuition," he does not ignore the quest of the scientist, his brother "born blind" as he was and "equipped with scientific tools." "The mystery is the same one. . . . As far as science pushes back its frontiers, and over all the stretched arc of these borders, the barks of the poet's pack of hounds will be heard."[12]

But this does not mean that the word "God" is indispensable to him in order to describe the mystery of reality. Claudel recognizes that if Saint-John Perse avoids it, he does so "religiously."[13] And the latter is grateful to his elder for having known how to insert the adverb in the friendly point of a literary eulogy. "It is only too true," he says, "that I must be scrupulous in forbidding myself to misuse a word which is today a mark of confessional acceptance, as long as the metaphysical concepts of absolute, eternity or infinity cannot, for me, coincide with the moral and personal concept which is the basis of the revealed religions. The quest for the divine in all things, which has been the secret tension of my entire life, and this intolerance in all things of the human limit, which continues to grow in me as a cancer, could in no way entitle me to more than my own aspiration. You are undoubtedly the only one who was able to grasp, in my poem, the scope of this 'Sea above the Sea' which always stretches beyond the line of my horizon."[14]

The previous year, Saint-John Perse had confessed his suffering to Claudel: "What could be more miserable, even more tragic, in its absurd contradiction, than this quenchless call to a spirituality that has neither object nor religious end; where everything in the human being, impatient with the human condition, is only useless irruption and attempt to break away from the human limits? . . . What a bitter enterprise, at the borders of the spirit, is this exploration without reconnoitering, these escapes without end, these issues without issue! I cannot retreat, I cannot resign myself, because I hate too much, with all my being, materialistic defeat. Rather then stick to this fatality in all things of a divine impregnation without access or recourse."[15] God is "the scattered" who "meets us in diversity."[16]

I believe that God is not scattered at all and that he is so personal that he has an infinite respect for this noble suffering; my own respect, spontaneous and reflected, is only a pale reflection of his. I do not want to give in to the panicky fear of anthropomorphism which is so common and so extreme in my contemporaries, even those who are Christians. Since this barbaric word is fashionable, I will take the liberty of being even more barbaric: God anthropomorphized himself so that man could be theomorphized, which means in everybody's language that God became man so that man could become God. There is no cheating in the Incarnation: God talks to men in the language of men; he does not expect men to talk about him and to talk to him in any language but their own. If the divine Word is a human word, the human word about God and to God is not *a priori* an alienation. It is clear that people should pay attention to the semantic evolution of words, and to the cultural context in which they are rooted. But this is another matter.

I am attacking here an obsession with mystification which is not a healthy one. Is this always the sign of a genuinely critical intelligence? It could just as well cover poorly disguised refusals. Just as there are cranks obsessed with suspicion and they are quite different from the great suspicious ones—Marx, Freud, Nietzsche—who had enough genius to give in one hundred years, as Mounier put it, three raps for attention to this civilization that was too secure in its balance. There are cranks obsessed with language who have only a remote resemblance to the seriously demanding minds that fight a just war against approximations and confusions. I shall not speak ill of concept in itself. How could one do without it? Poets are rightly wary of it, though they cannot eliminate it. They pull it away from the wear and tear of habit, they renew it, transfigure it; they do not reduce it to nothingness. Léon-Paul Fargue did say: "Let nothing argumentative infect your sense of God!", but then he corrected himself: "Poetry confides in reason: it trusts this dry, wise daughter who smells of an ant; it saved her from pernicious anemia and reason serves it well." Jesus was a great poet, the greatest of all poets, Poetry itself. I mean by this that he was the site of the Presence, adhesion to the Presence, unique experience of the inexpressible, unsharable intimacy with the living God whose essence is intimacy. Using everyday words, words translating concepts, he expresses this inexpressible, he shares with his brothers this unsharable. Why should I then become fussy when talking about God? I shall say: love, generosity, poverty, humility . . . Words? Concepts? Yes, but rescued from pernicious anemia if their original bond with the experience of Jesus has not been broken.

Indeed, concepts are often anemic. They are essential to the life of the spirit, but they do not constitute all the life of the spirit. They are often the least spiritual part of the spirit. Or, to put it in another way, they are the most exterior part of its interiority. They become truly anemic if they are left to their own devices without supervision: they play what are rightly called games of concepts! Born of concrete singularity, they boast of the universality and of the power of reflection to which they testify. But if they do not return to the concrete order, where is the advantage? How then could one prevent them from wilting? What is real is universal but it is concretely universal. Thus we must trust in concept and be wary of it. Reflection is already immanent to the hearing of God's word. There is not on one side the word of God in a pure state, and on the other, human reflection. A faith that would not in any way be conceptualized is nothing but a myth, which is really why the works of Saint Paul and Saint John have already the start of a theology. I refuse to suspect *any* theology of being the starting point of an ideology. But I do not disregard the danger: wanting to erect systems, the mind often demonstrates its own limitations.

Why should one reject without appeal the Thomistic doctrine of analogy? It is a deep one. It enables us to include a natural knowledge of God in the heart of the knowledge of faith, without any wall between the two of them. It protects us against this extrinsicism lucidly denounced by Blondel, which pays a suspicious homage to Revelation. The doctrine shows how the knowledge of God, received as a whole, is wholly ours: God is known only through God, but we are the ones who know him. Grace is inscribed in the very structure of the spirit. God honors his rational creature by predisposing it to receive the gift he makes of himself. This capacity to receive, which is itself given to us, is the very essence of reason. Therefore I have the right to be proud of being spirit. Such a pride cannot be dissociated from humility: such virtues are more metaphysical than moral and pay homage to the sovereign respect of God towards the autonomy—relative but real—of reason, his image. Undoubtedly there is quite a distance between the God of the philosophers and the God of Abraham, Isaac, Jacob and Jesus Christ. But it is the God of Abraham, Isaac, Jacob and Jesus Christ who, himself, refuses to cease being the God of the philosophers: such a refusal means that he takes man seriously and not only in his ultimate vocation and the transcendence of his end, but also in the depth of his implantation.

Thus I will say that God is humble, knowing that he cannot be so in the way men can and should be humble. The concept of humility—like those of wisdom, power or goodness—cannot by itself apply to anyone but the creature. There is no concept which can embrace infinite and finite, not even the concept of being. I cannot affirm anything about God, purely and simply. Negation must immediately pierce through affirmation: God is humble, God is not humble. More radically: God is, God is not. To extend unto infinity the meaning of a concept meant for the finite would insert God in the category of the finite, thus denying him, or in other words mythicizing him. Negation is a death I inflict on the concept in order for it to resurrect, other than what it had been, and capable of saying something true about God. In this vein, I dare talk about a paschal mystery of intelligence. Christians— and mystics especially—will be able to make use of it, understood and lived according to its Christic scope in the light of the Holy Spirit; though it is already present, at the root of the thinking being. There is nothing without death: intelligence does not escape this law of life. But negation, while it pierces through affirmation, does not abolish it, because it is impossible that God not be the source of all that is in the creature. There is a resemblance between the source and the river, but the source is quite different. What we say about the river is true of the source, though according to a superior mode of meaning, which is called "eminent" in classical vocabulary. God is humble; God is not humble; God is eminently humble. This eminent mode cannot be determined: it escapes us. "The extreme peak of the human knowledge of God," says Saint Thomas, "consists in knowing that God is unknown to us, in this that his proper being is beyond all that we understand."[17] And elsewhere: "We cannot grasp what God is, but what he is not, and what relationship sustains all the rest with him."[18] No concept *represents* God. Therefore there is not, to be rigorously logical, an analogy of concept. But there is a judgment of analogy which *means* God without representation, even an imperfect one.

Is it possible to think about God while rejecting *all* analogy? Many have tried it. I am afraid that it was futile. But I can understand well enough that a concern for logic could entail here some timidity and distrust. Rigorous logic and daring can only be combined if one recognizes the active presence of God from the very start of the reflection that leads to him. I must stress: not the idea of God, but God. And here again, the silent guitar of Doña Music beckons to us to warn us that the mysterious depth of man is indivisibly present and absent to self, memory of self, and memory of God, nostalgia and call. And that to start on the road to the Absolute even to the extent of aiming to reach his boundaries, means that one remembers him.

One should not be afraid of God. But to avoid being burned by his contact, we place between him and ourselves the screen of concept. Or rather, we are secretly glad that it is here in its opacity. It serves as a refuge, a haven, an armor. Even when purified, the idea of God protects us from God, since no intellectual purification would suffice to bare the being to its root: one needs the active and transforming Presence. In the same way, the idea of charity softens the demand of charity; the idea of freedom blunts the dart of freedom. Thus the fear of God leads to the fear of living and one winds up envying existences, be they individual or collective, that have no history: no thought, no initiative, no love. Could one desire, in order to vanquish fear, an intuition of God? If I question the mystics, who are witnesses to such a victory, I hear them warning me with severity. They speak of passivity, they ask me to beware of a privileged knowledge of God that would not be free of a spirit of ownership. Such a knowledge would be bending toward aestheticism: there would be a mirror at hand in which one could not help but contemplate himself, while believing that he is contemplating God. One would be watching this approach to privilege, and that would be the end of privilege. For the death implied in this approach is actual death only if one walks in the night.

Therefore there is no reason to pay too much attention to the noetic aspect of mysticism. Fénelon is right when he wants the desire for night to be mortified. It is good to nourish in oneself feelings that are quite friendly towards God—this is what being a man is, as Plato said—in order to be willing to stand and walk before him, naked, without support, without defense and security. But it can only be under the condition of not appropriating in advance the sacrifice of representation which is the very drive of the mystical impulse. That would be giving credit to oneself for the initiative, while in fact only God can achieve the spiritual about-face making such a sacrifice and such an impulse possible.

Men and women who have no pretense whatever are often the most moving witnesses of such an about-face to non-seeing and non-knowing. The fear of God has been exorcized in them through the faithful achievement of concrete acts commanded by duty. No big feats. They could not explain that if the will is the locus of union with God, it is because will is the deepest part of the being; but, endeavoring in simplicity to want in all things what God wills, they radiate—even in suffering and failure—trust, peace, joy. The conversion of heart—in the biblical meaning of the word—is also in them a conversion of intelligence. Taste for God and sense of God is all the same to them. They are better theologians than the theologian who is sitting tonight at their table; they interpret the Gospel more clearly than he does. He is hampered by the screen of ideas; they have no such problems. He came armed with concepts; he returns stripped of all but the unimpeachable Presence. Such encounters convince us that God affirms himself in the thread of life itself with a sovereign discretion, and that our affirmation is only an echo of his. At this point there is a deepening of what we suffer at being still separated from the beatific vision.

And one understands why the Eastern Christian theologians so strongly emphasize the degradation of the intellect that has been wounded by sin. To go from very simple experience to logical discourse, no matter how careful one is not to break the tie that must hold them together, can never be achieved without some deflowering. Is this because reflecting is a reflection, a remoteness from self, a look looking at itself? Whereas God . . . Let the questioning remain here a questioning, as one step on the road that leads to divine humility! But I do welcome, as a message that could be providential in these times when comprehension is often reduced to its calculating function, the invitation of Lossky, Evdokimov and Olivier Clément: not to exempt my intelligence from the baptismal death and resurrection. They tell me that intelligence is not only bound by its own limits: it is sinful. God honors it by healing it. Nothing here could smack of a suspicious antirationalism. One must provide for the evangelization of all our faculties.

A bright mind can coexist with darkness of the heart. Who has not suffered in feeling himself very far from self and God at the very moment he was enchanted by the discovery of depth in a dogmatic statement? The light is only a passing one: flashes of lightning follow flashes of lightning, but the night remains night: one slips into idolatry, one finds oneself in front of a god who is not God. "If then the light inside you is darkness, what darkness that will be!" (Mt 6:23). The distrust with regard to dogmas is growing apace, but this should not stop me from affirming their necessity. A tough job! The temptation, at times, is to escape from it lest one incline too much, through rationalistic rigidity and oblivion of mystery, towards a multiplication of misunderstandings. But that would be walking on the way of least resistance which sooner or later leads to the swamps.

Indeed, the dogmas protect us from the most dangerous of our dreams: the religious dreams, the ones we believe to be pure because they are about God. But none of our dreams are pure and we are deluding ourselves when we project upwards our noblest aspirations to erect—freely, as we believe—a God who might be greater than the God of Jesus Christ, and we do not see that we also project our sins at the same time. Let us listen to Nietzsche: "He who praises this God as the God of love does not have a high enough notion about love itself," and we flatter ourselves of conceiving, beyond the dogmas that are seemingly limiting, a love the elevation of which would be unmatchable. There is, doubtless, a need for much time and painful experience to realize that such a conception is beyond human reach. It is not possible to deny, even in thought, that even the most disinterested love entails a recoil upon the self, which mars it with selfishness. In our dreams, the Other is not other. We are pursuing the Same, in fact: ourselves. The God of pure subjectivity can only be a sinful projection of self. This is why dogmatic affirmation interrupts the fatal process. Through its very rationality, it guides us towards the spirit of childhood and forbids the property-seeking ego to rape the objective mystery. It blocks the gate to it. Even if such an affirmation were to seem guilty of trespassing!

It is at this point of reversal that we meet nowadays the many misconceptions which lend an appearance of health to this violent wind of antidogmatism sweeping almost the entire field of Christian experience. The use of the word "dogmatism," which is in a way exclusively disparaging, shows quite well that in many cases opposition and even repulsion toward what is dogmatic has to be interpreted as a healthy reaction. It is a visceral and reflected rejection of an intellectual despotism the boundaries of which have more than once been overstepped, as we well know. This is why many give in to the trend in order to reach a purer faith and a more committed responsibility. And here we meet delusion. If the Church has dogmas, it is so that no one be deluded about what love is. They can easily be accused of ideology: in fact, their purpose and necessary effect is to prevent love from becoming ideology. They seem triumphant: they are at the service of humble negative theology. They mark out its way. The paradox is that they are presented as affirmation, when their function is to set limits to a subjectivity gone mad, and to prevent it from affirming itself in its own drive. But this paradox is necessary, since mere formal negations would not lead to the riches of the Ineffable: the mystery would be reduced to an enigma, namely the disappearance of Reality itself.

The Church does not honor its God as a supreme professor who would expound his being in statements logically presented for the satisfaction of the mind. It does not impose with authority and in a wholly extrinsic way, theorems proudly demonstrated and presented as such that their knowledge would be necessary for salvation. It simply sees to it that the light of Christ, of which it is the sacrament, be correctly received at all times and everywhere. Such a concern leads the Church to formulate, at some point or other in history, its own experience so that the relationship of its sons with the living God not be perverted.

These formulations, achieved after a long and laborious reflection, also mark the start of a new reflection. They are a beginning more than they are an end. They enable all the brothers of Jesus Christ to recognize one another in the same adoration. Without a common tongue, anarchy will take over and lead to divisions. If the language becomes obsolete, nothing prevents us from renewing it while remaining faithful to the meaning it contains. One must go further and say: we must work at it because "faith is not a cry." Blondel wrote to Bremond: "Dogmatic theology suggests the divine secrets just as perceptions suggest the secrets of nature." I am confirming this phrase in connection with the humility of God: it is dogma—christological and trinitarian—which led me to go forth, in the opposite extreme to dogmatism, towards this secret of secrets which gives me light and nourishment.

Chapter Two

GOD REVEALED THROUGH DOING

God reveals what he is through what he does. His design for man, fulfilled in Jesus Christ, reveals his intimate being. One cannot separate act and being in him. The Incarnation is an act of humility because God is a being of humility. "To have seen me is to have seen the Father," says Jesus (Jn 14:9). When I see him humbly washing the feet of men, I thus see if he tells the truth, God himself eternally and mysteriously a Servant of humility in the very depth of his Glory. The humiliation of Christ is not an exceptional phase of glory. It demonstrates in time that humility is in the heart of glory. What I am stating here so calmly is such a strong paradox that reason first totters, abashed and as if disheartened at the outset. Yet, if one temporarily gives up concepts to their seeming contradiction, and chooses to refer directly to the experience one has of love—even love mingled with sin—a ray of light can already be seen through the night of the words. One perceives that love mixed with pride is not true love. If God is Love, he is humble.

A creature tends spontaneously to look for God as a Power. It is not possible to avoid such an approach. As a Christian called to contemplate the absolute Powerlessness of a crucified Christ, the creature clings stubbornly to the first approach which marked it so deeply. Poorly converted, it wavers between two images of divinity that it hopelessly tries to reconcile since they cannot be unified: that of the pagan and domineering Power remains unchanged under the Christian Powerlessness, agonizing and dying, superimposed on top of it. Such a coexistence is disastrous for both the soul and the mind. Indeed, God is Almighty. But what is his power? It is the All-Powerlessness of Calvary that reveals the true nature of the All-Power of the infinite Being. The humility of love is the key: to show off, there is little need of power; to efface oneself one must be very powerful. God is unlimited Power of self-effacement.

Two men helped me to understand that humility is the expression of the highest value: the philosopher Jean Nabert, and the theologian Romano Guardini. I must stress that for Nabert, the divine is that which qualifies certain human acts or beings insofar as they go beyond the order of ethics: such an approach to the absolute does in no way imply an affirmation of God. I am accepting here, without any extrapolation, the precision and truly spiritual elevation of an analysis.[19] Here is a man who gives up the exercise or the defense of a right: he is not compelled to do so through circumstancial necessity. He also renounces affectionate ties that would have been a source of joy for him: nothing forces him to do so. He even gives up the fostering of certain talents that would have increased his social power and fame while enriching his inner life: a beautiful and free flowering which does not violate any moral imperative. Such a renunciation is pure humility. Pure? It would not be so, were it sought or wanted as such, if any complacency were to twist it into a concern for exemplary virtue, if it were inspired by timidity or an obscure feeling of unworthiness or a hidden fear of failure. But such is not the case at all. It is pure, meaning "fully spontaneous and in accordance with the most secret powers of conscience, with the certainty that there is in all desire to worth, per se, an element of vanity and self-love or the wish to be greater than another being . . . "

No system of ethics denies that man, in his social life, must have rights and must claim respect for them. These rights are themselves established upon a general right to have rights. And in the last analysis, this right is based on faith in reason, namely: in man. No one, therefore, can compel anybody into a renouncing humility. That could only be done by undermining the necessary legal order. Humility is not a duty. It cannot even be recommended. On the ethical level, it is ambiguous: it often destroys the individual, unless he is hypocritical in his practice of it. The most that can be asked of him is that he moderate pride or presumption. But that would be a minimization and would pervert its essential meaning. In truth, humility witnesses to a radical move beyond the order of morality. The meaning or the idea of humility is distorted when one debases the worth of the being of whom it is the act. On the contrary, one must think that humility reaches its fullness only when it is linked to the highest conceivable worth of which it is, as it were, the supreme expression. In this sense, it is divine. It is then impossible for a believer not to credit God with it.

One must also call divine the love which is strong enough not to demand reciprocity as a condition for its constancy. Being steeped in humility, it remains equal to itself in spite of the vacillations of the beloved's response. "The desire for God," says Nabert, "is nothing less than the desire for a being whose love for us would go radically beyond our unworthiness and the waverings of our love for him." God, if he exists, is this Being who utters an "I love you" without conditions. Only he can do so: love, in our world, cannot last and perdure without a minimum of reciprocity. The men and women who have loved without being loved know that they have not loved enough not to be prey to the temptation of despair and even suicide. In God, one cannot separate intensity and purity of love. Intensity: the power to go to the very limits of self, madness—

manikos eros—as Cabasilas said. Purity: the humility of not claiming anything for self.

"What God," asks Guardini, "reveals himself in this Jesus, who fails so dreadfully, who finds no other companions than these fishermen, who is defeated by a caste of political theologians, who is brought to justice and condemned as a visionary and revolutionary?" It is difficult to believe that all that happens in this life happens in God. Yet one must do so, at least if one accepts without any arbitrary reduction the unheard-of expression related by Saint John: "Whoever has seen me has seen the Father." But reason cannot avoid the obstacle of incomprehension if it does not give up the notion it had of God before knowing Jesus Christ. Christology is not superimposed on a preceding theology; it is theology which is rooted in christology. Thus Guardini asks the real question: "Jesus, being what he is, his life unfolding before us as we see it, how is the God who reveals himself in it?" In other words: "How can God be in order to give to himself such an existence?" The answer is given in Scripture: God is Love. But in love there is something that we do not perceive right away: humility.

To bow before the greatness of another is not, properly speaking, humility. It is only loyalty, honesty, truth, politeness of the mind. When a smaller being pays homage to a greater one, this is not the proof of an exceptionally noble soul. When the greater one, however, bows respectfully before the smaller one, this points to love in the fullness of its freedom and riches. Francis of Assisi is not humble when he kneels before the Pope, but only when he bows before a poor man in whose poverty he recognizes the robes of majesty. His gesture is not condescending; his look is not overbearing. There is no constraint: spontaneity is absolute, it expresses love just as breathing signifies life. One must be immensely great to breathe in such a manner. One must be God. The humility of Francis is a participation in the humility of his Lord.[20] Holderin used as a head-ing for his *Hyperion* the well-known sentence of a young XVIIth century Flemish Jesuit: *Non coerceri maximo, contineri tamen a minimo, divinum est.* "It is a divine thing not to be held by the greatest and yet to be contained in the smallest." There may not be a more beautiful expression of the Christian conception of God's greatness. But I dare go further than the opposition: to be contained in the smallest constitutes the greatness that nothing can hold.

Humility is the most radical aspect of love. Poverty, understood in a purely spiritual sense, is not perfectly synonymous with it. There is a slight nuance which should not be overlooked. The concept of poverty is originally connected with the order of having. It is transposed to that of being, in which it acquires a new meaning. Yet, it retains the memory of its former signification. It is not possible to quiet its echo successfully. So that words such as "proud poverty" do not suffer much from being uttered in one breath, unless one means "humility" when saying "poverty." Poverty, in itself, does not denote a lack of recoil on self, a selfish withdrawal, even if it is ordinarily understood as such in the field of spiritual life. Humility, born in the order of being, without any connection with that of having, is the soul of poverty. Which is why Osty translates beautifully the first evangelical beatitude: Blessed are those who have the soul of the poor. The word "poor" is kept because of the tie which is constant in the Old Testament and has not been destroyed in the New Testament, between the two meanings of the word: economical and spiritual. "Soul" denotes a step beyond in interiority.

It is permitted to spiritually qualify the ontological attributes of God. Perhaps one must do so, if it is believed that there is no point in seeking the understanding of his mystery in any other way than that of love. Love is more than being. In the same way one says that Mozart is Music made man, I dare say that God is the hypostatized spiritual Life. Beyond the distinctions between being and non-being, finite and infinite, contingent and necessary, there is an abysmal depth of God that we would not betray so crudely, in my opinion, if we were to attempt an approach in terms of spirituality. Just as there are in the language of the Scholastics, transcendentals of the being, as such, nothing prevents us from conceiving transcendentals of the spiritual being, meta-ontologicals, so to speak.

If God is invisible, it is certainly because he is Spirit and immanent to us. This is ontological. But it is also—and here is the spiritual part—because he is to us more intimate than the most intimate of ourselves. "Intimate" means—as "immanent" cannot do—that God embraces the soul in love. He is the Other, but not remote. He is hidden. Humbly hidden, for we could not see him and remain free. The invisibility of God is his humble respect for our freedom. There is no such thing as proud fullness. How could one imagine a God full of himself? He would be a Croesus satisfied with his wealth. His being would be for him a having. Idol for himself. Therefore idol for his creature who would be nothing more than an extension of himself.

God is Excess of love, which means that he is not narcissistically watching himself in the process of exceeding love. This mystery was suggested to me by music. The fullness of Bach, and that of Mozart are also without pride: they signs without listening to themselves singing. But the prodigious Wagnerian symphony, even at its summits, shows disturbing signs: the man of Bayreuth knows, and it is evident, that he is a demi-god. It is difficult to prevent imagination from wandering. One could easily replace the rejected image of an infinite Narcissus admiring himself and being enchanted by himself, with the phantasm of a timid, withdrawn, pallid being, to the extent that he might be ashamed of being God and willing to give up the absolute. It is something to beware of. Flamboyant or baroque glory does efface itself but only in the disappearance of all glory. The notion of a humility that would be the confession of something missing or of a necessity, can intrude absurdly. This is only another form of idolatry.

One should also beware of aesthetic humility. God has none of this heady modesty on which Gide confesses that he got drunk at times. No enjoyment of being incognito. Some men enjoy their own weakness just as others enjoy their own strength. There are those who seek failure. Such doubtful phantasms have to be swept aside when one thinks about God. It is difficult to forgive a man for being better than we are, no matter in what respect, unless he is humble. If he is, all is changed: his superiority is at the same time cancelled and confirmed. Cancelled in this, that it does not threaten to cancel us. Confirmed, because it is sealed with humility. One cannot be jealous of a humble great person. Jesus commands us not to call our brother a fool. Though there are people who can do so without uttering a word. Their bearing is humiliating. A humble person does not humiliate: the depth of his being does not allow it. So is God in his transcendence.

The most admired writers are not always the most beloved ones. When we love in friendship, as if he lived nearby, a poet or a novelist whose works enchant us, the heart and the mind receive a precious happiness. But such a wonder is fragile! It is enough to detect, at the bend of a sentence or a verse, a hint of pride for the wonder to start wilting. I love Claudel in friendship as much as I admire him because I have gleaned in the field of his work, especially in his *Journal*, many clear signs of humility. In 1900, the arms of Ysé had stifled his young pride: he recognized in her the great humiliating one. I have never been bothered by what remained in him of a superficial vanity. For he felt that this was a shortcoming. He was not of those of whom Péguy writes, "they almost lack." Many were fooled: they admire Claudel, but cannot love him. Péguy himself said: "(I) hate a humility that would not be a Christian humility, that would be a species of civil, civic, lay humility . . . a substitute humility," and at that level he saw himself as chock-full of pride; and how could we love him in friendship if we did not discern in him, clearly for those who know how to read him, a genuine humility?

And so it is, not only for the writers who are dear to us, but for the heroes they created. We love in friendship the prideless priests of Bernanos. We love in friendship this Vera Ganger whose face and soul were fervently sculpted by Solzhenitsyn, and so many others. . . . If God were not humble, how could we have for him these "friendly feelings" that Plato deems essential to man? The experience of human love is the least inadequate to suggest love such as it is lived in God. For even if still very natural and such that one can describe its components in a simply phenomenological way, it is already moving towards its ultimate end; it is—at its very root—a desire to love as God loves, and a capability of being transfigured by the Spirit into the achievement of its vocation.

It certainly remains very far from the absolute disinterest of divine love, but however mingled it be with a selfish passion that encapsulates it, one can perceive in it a light, which in the dimness of its morning, is none other than that of the eternal sun. There are no two suns: there are no two loves. If human love can lead to divine love, it is because the former is a manifestation of the latter, even if it has no inkling yet of its nobility and does not know that it will have to be transfigured, which is why I can invite the fiancé, the husband, or the friend, to listen to the best of his heartbeats: he will then hear an echo of God's heartbeat. Love is poverty, dependence, humility. The lover tells the beloved: "You are my joy." This is an affirmation of poverty: without you I am poor of joy. Or else: "You are all to me." This is the affirmation of my nothingness outside of you. To love is to want to be *through* the other and *for* the other. *Through* the other: a welcome. *For* the other: a gift. Both aspects pertain to poverty.

In humanly lived love, what restricts the desire to welcome and to give is the claim to self-sufficient wealth, thus mutilation of love. In our world, every love is more or less maimed. But there is in any love, enough love for us to sense what love is when it is only love, when nothing limits its power to welcome and to give: it is poverty. The relationships of the three Persons are relationships of poverty. God is absolutely Poor. One cannot say in the same breath: "I love you" and "I want to be independent of you." The one cancels the other. In love, one wants to be dependent: "I shall follow you to the end of the world." The most loving is the most dependent. An infinity of love is an absolute, I would not say of dependence—because one could not avoid understanding this in the ontological meaning and that would be a contradiction in terms—but of the desire to depend. If love is not an aspect of God but God himself, the desire to depend qualifies his being.

This dependence is not the result of a need, such as the need of a child for its mother: it is pure tension towards the other, or attention to the other, such as that of the mother towards the child. If one does not take seriously the purity of love in God, if one persists in imagining that he is a being unconverted to love, the paradox dissolves itself into absurdity. It is not possible to look down on someone to whom we say: "I love you." The overbearing look would reduce love to nothingness. This is clear in the case of contempt. But it is already true if the lover, greater in some way than the beloved, does not deny radically in the very act of loving whatever superiority he has. Wordless denial, which is all in the eyes. A look meaning: "I am more than you are" cannot mean: "I love you."

What power has God, whose love has no condescension! A power which is an unfathomable mystery. Jesus reveals it to us when he washes the feet of his disciples, without feint or pretense: his gesture truly tells us how God loves. If the paradox remains really too strong and if our reason, incapable of conceiving an infinity of poverty, dependence and humility, cannot prevent itself from protesting, there is another way to suggest the mystery: God is infinitely rich. But he is rich in love, not in having nor in being possessed as an asset. Riches in love is synonymous with poverty. God is sovereignly independent, therefore free. But he is free to love and to go to the extreme of love. The extreme of love is renunciation of independence; at the limit, it is death. "A man can have no greater love than to lay down his life for his friends." God is immensely great and powerful. But his greatness is to be able to do all that love does, even to self-effacement in the humility of the eyes.

In other words, God is such that his riches, his freedom, his power—riches of love, freedom of love, power of love—can only be (and are in fact) translated, expressed, revealed in the poverty, the dependence and the humility of Jesus Christ. If, on the one hand, I do not know Jesus Christ, if on the other hand, I have no experience of love, friendship or charity, nothing could be more mysterious; all becomes an enigma. And how sad it is! It would be better to avoid imagining how God looks at man. I use the word "imagining" because, in truth, this is just an image. But how can we abolish it? It survives critical effort. One can hardly rid himself of its crudest forms: the spying look, the annulling one, the one making an object or a spectacle out of man, the one freezing his liberty. Even if one succeeds in doing so, there remains a look that still bothers only a few people, though it troubles Kirillov, the hero of *The Possessed* until madness: the look which simply looks.

Kirillov is an imaginary person, but Guardini showed very well how his case reveals that of Nietzsche, in the way pathology often unveils the springs and orientation of a normal sensitivity. A proud being cannot tolerate being raped in his most private self by the look of another, even if this other be God. "What anguishes Kirillov is not a particular reason such as, for instance, the fear of being guilty; but he feels before the gigantic shadow of the other the anguish of a finite and fragile existence, aspiring to the fullness of life and claiming its freedom and dignity; he has the feeling of being chased away from the depth of his innermost self, raped in his dignity and modesty."

Nietzsche expresses himself in the same vein: the look of God strips him "of his humanity and his honor." God anguishes man. He is the anguish of man. He must be made to disappear, for "if I must be, he cannot be. Yet, I must be: therefore he must not be."[21] If God were the other as merely other, Kirillov and Nietzsche—and today Jean-Paul Sartre—would be right. It would be a duty to affirm atheism as a postulate for freedom. It would be only legitimate defense. But the God of Christian faith is not that other who is counted together with his creatures. He is not even the All Other. He is All-Otherly other, thus just as well Non-Other. However, I am not identical to him: he is not the Same. Neither Other nor Same. But Transcendence of love implying otherness and being more immanent to me than my own immanence. While reason exhausts itself in trying to purify its concepts, the image of the look persists in spite of everything. And what of it! Unable to destroy it, I welcome its tenacity if at least it is clothed in a radiant humility. Then there is no more danger.

Only God is humble. Man is not so, except in the fact that he admits being unable of humility. Here, one must go step by step. At the outset, humility is a respect for the values of which we are aware. Justice and beauty are in us, they are ourselves and they are not us. They are not futile abstractions, and even in order to be, they must be manifested in actions that are just or beautiful—in this sense, one must say that reason invents them—it is also true that they are grasped as a *given*, namely, that they are received. They have authority. To respect this authority is in itself humility. When God reveals himself as a personal Being, living, and dwelling inside consciousness, there is in me not only something which is other than me, but Someone who is in me more myself than me. Then humility crosses a threshold. The *given* comes from a *Giver* "whom I serve" (1 K 17:1). To recognize is not only to know, or to admit, at the level of impersonal values; it is to praise, thus already to love. It is my Creator who gives me the ability to create. There is an initiative preceding mine and superior to it, without which I would have no power of initiative. Someone gives me the ability to possess myself as a mind and as a freedom. There is a Source without which I would not be a source, a light that sets me afire. There is a creative gratuitousness. Respect of values has become a loving respect for God. Another threshold is crossed when Christ reveals the Creator as a Father who divinizes his creatures and calls them his children (1 Jn 3:1). Then humility becomes an active welcome of God known not only as *Giver* but as *Self-Giver*. The Privacy of God opens itself before us to let us enter *into* him: one does not exist *before* him; "in him we live, we move, we are" (Ac 17:28) and Christ is "in the Father" (Jn 14:10). Here, humility is reduced to stammering, abashed poverty, wordless admiration of the immensity of Love.

The third threshold is the recognition of the immensity of love as an immensity of humility. It is at this point that the humility of man admits its failure. It will be only at the end of his itinerary, when Purgatory will have finally reduced to nothingness—as Blondel says—"the nothingness that he is" that man will be able to love as God loves, to be humble as God is humble. As long as we walk on earthly roads, humility, though always seen as necessary, must be understood as being far beyond our reach. For the instinct of ownership does not avoid seizing upon it as an object which it enjoys, clothes it with vanity as it takes root and grows, and thus destroys it. Only God, by making us aware of the fact that we cannot be humble, makes us humble. The victory of humility can only be the confession of its defeat.

One only has to question the saints. All of them, to various degrees, had undertaken to achieve perfection by sculpting their own statue. All of them had to give this up sooner or later, when God enlightened them on their powerlessness to stop watching themselves grow in perfection. Without such a renunciation they would not be saints. For it is not in the order of *having* that appropriation is the most radically opposed to love. More dangerous and more subtle is appropriation in the order of *being* and *acting*: ownership of self, and especially of one's moral progress. Just as a coquette looks into her mirror, sees herself becoming beautiful and is enchanted by the artificial increase of her beauty, the soul strives and becomes proud of its own striving. The "nothingness that we are" withdraws on itself.

But God unfolds it and in so doing, reduces it to nothingness. His active presence unglues us from ourselves, and in proportion to our abandonment to him, purifies us of all ownership instinct. The humility of a perfectly "unfolded" God destroys that which in our necessary aspiration to humility is destructive of humility. He achieves that which we are powerless to achieve by ourselves: breaking the mirror in front of which we were working at stripping ourselves of pride, while being satisfied of the stripping. Then, we don't know anymore whether we are humble. We only know, as Simon Peter by the lake (Jn 21:15), that is enough for God to know and to want more from us. We walk in life as a joyful child for whom all is light, except himself.

Saint Augustine distinguished three degrees in love: *amare amari*, to love being loved; *amare amare*, to love to love; *amare*, to love. Humility is absent in the first two degrees. It gives its purity to the third one. "Fénelon," writes Vladimir Jankelevitch, "advised the lover to love not *in order to love*, but *for the sake of the beloved*: *Amare amatum* and not *amorem*—since love is meant not to love itself with a half-baked and unnatural love, a shameful love, a black love, but to love its beloved with a successful love; a love that comes back to itself in a closed circle is a sad failure of love: but the subject of love who runs straight to the object of love reaches the infinitely remote otherness of the non-me; the love of this subject is successful."[22] The preceding lines announce our future themes of God's simplicity (in the etymological meaning of the word) and of his infinite distance with regard to himself.

To be loved by a very humble person is very touching. I am overwhelmed with an invincible sweetness by a look which, as I can clearly see, is not attached to itself but comes to attach itself to me. I hardly dare respond, so poignant is the question it asks. Sweetness and pain together, as in the deepest songs of Mozart. At first I have the feeling of something inaccessible which, at the very moment it offers itself to me, remains inaccessible. However, if I give in little by little, my emotion is most intense when I see that my response is accepted. How deeply am I then aware of my unworthiness! As we go along, I will have to control tears of contrition. I believe that it was Gide who said that Bach's music is a music of contrition, since it gives us the feeling of what we constantly fail to achieve.

Is man intolerably arrogant when he believes that there can be, between his God and himself, a real exchange based on a tie of actual reciprocity? Many rebel against what they consider to be no more than a naive pride. Not so Bergson. "A saint," he said, "draws no pride from his elevation. On the contrary, his humility is great. How could he not be humble when he has been able to encounter, in silent conversations, face to face, moved by a feeling in which his whole soul was melting, what could be called the divine humility?"[23] There is no false sentimentality in such an emotion. Scripture, the Fathers of the Church and the mystics do not hesitate to talk about the faith of God. The idea of a Covenant is fundamental: in it, God gives his faith and asks man to give his own in exchange. If he responds, he is worthy, says Saint Cyril of Jerusalem, "to be called by the same name as God." They are both faithful. Saint John of the Cross goes so far as to talk about the "faith of the two parties."[24] To give one's faith, is to make a commitment of dependence; fidelity is life lived in such a dependence. There is certainly no contradiction between freedom and dependence, since the dependence into which God wants to enter reveals the true nature of his freedom, and that of ours too, which is the image of his.

Thus, one shall not say that by becoming dependent of a nature, through the incarnation God lessens himself. To the contrary, he shows what it is to be God. Bulgakov says that "he aligns himself on the inferior." This is a daring phrase, but it does not mean that God abdicates his transcendence. Rather, it calls us to understand that it would be by enclosing himself in his own transcendence that God would be abdicating it. A solipsistic enclosure in love is a contradiction in terms. This does not mean that one must follow Angelus Silesius, who in his extreme audacity, let it be thought that the reciprocity of the creature is a need for God. Yet, we will affirm with him that the Creator is truly hungry and thirsty for the love of his creature. Not that he *needs it*: God is absolutely self-sufficient; He is God independently of the world. Though he is vulnerable: "God is wounded by nothing," but, "one can wound God."[25]

These two propositions are formally in contradiction. However, one can get over such a contradiction by admitting that the will is the most divine trait of God, just as it is the most human characteristic of man. God is what he wants to be. At the beginning is the Gratuitousness of freedom. Moreover,

Christ reveals to us that in his beatitude, God does not want to do without us. He is vulnerable because he wants to be so; but for him, to want to be is to be.

When it comes to God, the word "love" is at the same time the most necessary and the most dangerous. The danger is to stop half-way when we explore its meaning: it can then cover all kinds of evasions, and hide many intellectual slips into confusion, or spiritual ones into sentimentality. When Saint John says and repeats in his first Epistle "God is Love" (1 Jn 4:8, 16), one must understand with Tradition that love is not *an* attribute of God which, even though it were the first, would be one attribute among his others. What the apostle affirms is that love is subject: to say God is to say Love. The attributes of God are then the attributes of love: it is love which is almighty, wise, free, good, and beautiful. Thus there is at the same time a continuity with and a break from the revelation of the Old Testament in that of the New. Nothing that was in the Old has been cancelled, but all has been transfigured from the roots up.

Indeed, the names given to God by the Old Testament would be pregnant with misunderstanding, if they were not understood in the light of the Gospel as preludes to the supreme unveiling, and therefore as already an unveiling. For experience and reflection show on the one hand that power, wisdom, goodness, etc., are genuine greatness only if they pertain to love; and on the other hand, that love itself is great only if it is powerful, wise, good, etc. Thus two errors must be avoided: to ignore that love is not an attribute but a subject; to deprive the subject of its essential attributes. Is humility an attribute of love? One could say so. But it is so deeply within the subject itself, that it is—certainly not its exact synonym—more than an aspect of it, its very depth. I will attempt to show that if humility is lacking, the attributes of God are "decomposed," deprived of their salt and savor, so to speak.

THE MOST HIGH—One cannot evade the naivety of one image by using another image belonging to the same category. It is not much better to prefer a concept. The metaphor of height suggests transcendence, while that of depth, immanence. But these very concepts in their abstraction are themselves affected with a spatial character. Léon Brunschvicg was certainly not deceived by the artificial antithesis he placed between imagination in height and reflection in depth. Images and concepts must equally be criticized if we do not want to be deceived, be it crudely or subtly. The mystics were not deceived when they spoke of the apex, summit, peak, or depth of the soul—*apex, acies, acument mentis, intimum, supremum.*

The spiritual experience by itself—and already that of human love up to a certain point—enables one to use the concrete image of height without any danger of spatial extrinsicism. But it is necessary to remember here that there are such states of extremely fine sensitivity in which the coexistence of contraries borders on the inexpressible. The look of love is not overbearing to the beloved. It could not survive a declaration, no matter how weak, of superiority. It is humble. But in humility itself, greatness is unveiled. This is why the respect proven by the humility of the lover arouses in the heart of the beloved another respect, effect and sign of another humility. Since there is no shadow of pride on the pupil of the lover's eye, his gaze seems—to the beloved—to be coming from very far, very *high*, from a world devoid of opacity, gravity, withdrawal into oneself.

The deeper the intimacy, the wider the distance. The humility of wonderment responds to the humility of loving ability. When it comes to God, the word "adoration" must be used. The creature, tightly embraced and embracing, adores from the depths the humility of the Immense who encloses himself in the minute, the highness of the Most High whose

3

heart is beating against its heart. Adoration is a mouth-to-mouth—*ad os*—in which the breaths are united in a different respect originating in a different humility. The Most High! How could one pronounce these two syllables without tenderness when one knows that God is nowhere else than in our most intimate self and in the communion of our brothers? And how could I dare be tender with him without the respect inspired in me by his respect?

GLORY—It is the appearance of the being, his manifestation. If the being is a source of light, glory is glowing, flaming, radiant. Thus Saint-John Perse, being at sea one night, saw the white clouds around an island "widely transpierced by a beam of luminous swords that in the language of other centuries the old master engravers used to call 'glory.' " The word, richly harmonious, works as a charm in poetry when Baudelaire or Mallarmé, for instance, tear it away from banality amd situate it intelligently within their verse. Human glory is ambiguous, pure or impure depending on the case. In itself, it means fame, self-aggrandizement, noise about the name, success, prestige, triumph, public consecration. This is often mistaken, because it happens that in the heart of such a superficial glory one can perceive a basic mediocrity, especially when clear signs point to a fame that has been sought, wanted for its own sake and delighting the one who obtained it. When the glittering mask is ripped off, a ridiculous vacuum is seen; from Plautus to Destouches, this has supplied much material for comedy. Contempt—smiling or not—goes with it: soldier or earl, a fig on the "glorious one"!

Quite removed from such a mockery, history does offer us pure glories. Pure? To a certain extent only since it is rare for the appearance not to inflate the being, to hypertrophy it unduly, thereby twisting it. The great men are not great in all respects. Having always corrupts value in some way, and it is hard to imagine how one could totally avoid possessing glory as wealth. Péguy was not wrong in thinking "that there is always some impurity in success, some crudeness in victory . . . a residual impurity in fortune . . . and that only defeat . . . is totally pure . . . totally great." There are not many great people who are humble. Those who toil at their work without caring for glory are, most of the time, victims of their contemporaries' injustice and history is slow at avenging them. At least, they remained pure. Unless they suffered excessively and not without bitterness, of the ingratitude and obscurity in which they were left to live and work! Here we reach the superior limit of man: candor can never be absolutely equal to worth.

The glory of God, transcending all limits, is his sanctity. The Bible makes no clear difference between the one and the other. This is fullness of being, its intensity, density, weight. If sanctity is the very substance of fire, glory is what we find intolerable and fascinating in it. It is at the same time the frontier of the heart of the being and the unveiling over the whole earth of his most intimate secret. Therefore, it is mobile, and if it were possible to suggest something a bit daring, one would have to unite paradoxically lightness and gravity, eagle and basalt, dance and column. All the strength and aerial grace contained in what we call Beauty. Terrible and ravishing all in one. Rilke, in the first *Elégie de Duino*, trembled before the Angels, living expressions of Glory:

> Who then, if I cried out, would hear me
> amid the hierarchy of the angels?
> And even if one of them suddenly
> were to hold me to his heart,
> his being would be too strong and I would perish.
> For what is beautiful is but the start of
> what is terrible, what we can hardly stand.
> And if we admire him so, it is because
> he will not condescend to destroy us.

All angels are terrible.
Better be silent about the obscure rise of the call.

The poet quieted his cry because he did not feel that the fascination is stronger than the trembling. The ancient Jews had felt it, but did they know the reason? It is because in God, there is a Glory beyond glory: the glory of wanting to be only love. It is there that humility is rooted, as Eckhart says. Glory is "weight": this is the first meaning of the Hebrew word *kabod*. But this is not the weight of a having, nor even the weight of self possessing self. Shall we say—and this is stammering—the spiritual weight eternally born of the lightening of the weight of self? In one word: the weight of love. By his incarnation and death, God renounces glory, but reveals the Glory that is beyond glory. For such an abyss, there are no more images, concepts, or words, even biblical ones. But instead we have the "evidence" of the Cross.

ALMIGHTY—One needs a long experience, perhaps a whole lifetime, to start understanding that in the order of love, just as riches are poverty, power is weakness. Man always tends when he thinks about his God, to go out of the sphere of love, to imagine attributes that would not be those of love. It took centuries to finally adore God not as the God of the armies but as the disarmed God. This is a classical pun and it means exactly what it expresses; it is wonderfully apt to show the pedagogy of Revelation. Just as there is a Glory beyond glory, there is a Power beyond all power. If Rilke had known this, he would not have spoken of the angels "not condescending" to destroy. He would have said "powerless." For love does not have the power to destroy what it creates; it does not have to control itself in order not to do it. The All-Power of God is the extreme opposite of the *potentia* that men imagined in their original weakness and to which, in the riches and strength they have now acquired, they take exception because they see it as a competing force. Humility competes with nothing. It is, at the fine point of power, this vulnerability of a child lying in a manger and of a young man nailed to a cross. Why must it be, when we pray liturgically to "Almighty and eternal God," that we have such trouble remembering the words of Jesus: "Who has seen me has seen the Father"? There is no other God than the Father of Jesus.

OMNISCIENT—Error here is dangerous: if God knows everything—past, present, future—how can one escape fatalism? His knowledge freezes my liberty. No matter how hard I put the brakes on my wandering imagination, I will not be able to erase from its horizon this high-perched observatory on which God stands motionless, looking over and watching the entire surface of seas and plains, puppet theater of the human comedy of which he knows—from all eternity (as the saying goes)—the beginning, the ups and downs, and the end. What is left to the actors, but to try and act well? And to stress the most offensive feature of the caricature, how can one avoid perceiving on the divine lips a smile of proud irony: "They don't know! I, God, I know!"? To affirm then that God is love will not only not remedy anything, but it leads to rebellion and refusal, because such a love cannot be loved.

The twisted image is tenacious, and there are many—though boasting of being philosophers—who do not cease being affected by it in the back of their minds, even if it has been chased away from the front. The image was born when I transposed in God my knowledge made asset, without any change. I know that the sum of all I know is only partial, but I thought that it was total in God. In me, it is limited, finite: in him, unlimited, infinite. I used my imagination to expand my knowledge and erase the borders into which it runs, and I said: God knows no counties, no river banks, no time, no space: omniscience. The fruit of this imagination is a phantasm of a knowing God who pretends to dialogue with his creature, but who, in truth, converses only with himself. My fault was in my inability to perceive in myself a disconnection, a gap between knowledge and love or, to use the language of certain philosophers, between mind and soul. There lies the human limit: to be able to know without loving and love without knowing.

Knowledge without love is this gaze of the mind upon itself which stops the leap of the soul. "The light of a thought that stops to know and to know itself can only issue from a broken momentum: mind. One must start again: soul."[26] But the soul can only start again if it gives up the pleasure of the game of the mind and the test of its power, and its advance is at first a groping in the dark. The mind then enlightens it, but again in folding back upon itself. The unity of knowledge and love, forever sought, is never reached. Such a process must be denied when we affirm the omniscience of love in God. In him, there is no break between the act of loving and the act of knowing. He is not mind and soul, but, transparent to himself without watching himself, he knows everything without anything being a spectacle for him. To say that he does not know that he knows would be equivocating and even, in itself, a falsehood. But what constitutes the mystery of God's humility is that in him the simplicity (in the etymological meaning: without fold) of the loving approach is devoid of all that the human way of knowledge implies in narcissism, even in its highest and most disinterested workings.

BEAUTY—We cannot say anything direct about the beauty of God, since what we call beauty is connected with sensitivity, and God such as he is in himself is "what eye has not seen, what ear has not heard." Moreover, just as in our experience there is a gap between knowledge and love, there is also another one between love and beauty. The meaning of art is linked with the dynamism of the mind itself: to restore the lost unity, to seek for the original identity. Péguy aims for this coincidence of aesthetics and ethics when he expresses in terms of moral values "the classical landscape at its peak of beautiful and ripe maturity." It is, as he puts it, "a just landscape . . . an equitable landscape . . . a good landscape. But not of this odious goodness which is nothing more than weakness . . . softness . . . falling of deliquescence. Good of this just goodness, daughter of justice, daughter of soundness, of this firm goodness, daughter of just firmness. The only really good one . . . Nothing but strength. Sweet landscape; only insofar as it is firmness which is the basis of the only true sweetness . . . Neither this hateful weakness that would make us hate goodness itself. Nor this odious harshness that would make us hate firmness itself."27

Nothing prevents us here from replacing "landscape" with "God": the predicates of beauty are the same as those of love. Which is why, notes Arthur Lourié in his *Journal musical*: "melody is tied in an elusive manner with morals. It has a peculiarity of a moral-aesthetic order which is one of the signs characteristic of melody's presence. . . . It may be that today we do not compose any more good melodies simply because we have become very nasty. In fact, there could not be a nasty melody. A nasty melody is an absurdity."28 However, beauty in our world is not love, even if it is a beautiful thing to love and if there is no beauty without some degree of love. Neither Péguy nor Lourié uses the word "humility." It is true that what they say implies it, but I, for one, want to recognize it explicitly. For humility is, in my opinion, one of the essential attributes of Beauty, at least the one which enables me to correct best the clumsy images I spontaneously have of God's beauty. A reasonable being cannot be proudly beautiful. If it is self-satisfied, beauty is immediately tarnished, imbued with the sense of ownership; it hurts itself with the dart of its own eyes, and is then unable to inflict the wound of love on the one who contemplates it, while innocent beauty is always poignant.

Marcel Proust speaks of "these young girls who, in a glance, seem to put between themselves and you this distance that their beauty makes painful." What would it be if the humility in the glance of these young girls were to put a distance between them and themselves! The Virgin of Moissaic opened a way for me towards the beauty of God. She flees to Egypt. She is sitting on a donkey—which seems to have escaped from a Supervielle tale—who seems very surprised to know whom he is carrying and very concerned to be worthy of her. Mary is a young peasant girl with the face of a doll lit from within by a music which is more earthly than celestial, a village song that she probably is humming. She bears a crown on her forehead, but it is so naively put on that she probably does not even know it is there; otherwise, she would certainly have straightened it. The child places his hand at the top of her blouse; she holds his left arm. Each gesture gives, in a holy manner, to the other gesture "the chord of the necessary note." Looking at this group as a child would look at his toy, is enough to assure us that a God who would not be humble could not give anyone the desire to sing.

MAJESTY—Rereading Pascal, I imagine that Vincent de Paul when he was in the presence of Louis XIV bowed before the royal majesty (because it is foolish and mean of spirit to refuse the established greatness what is its due), while the king bowed interiorly before the majesty of the saint. Two different types of majesty arousing two different types of respect. When it comes to the majesty of God, it is only the contemplation of Jesus Christ that can prevent imagination from wandering. A long and deep recollection is needed, for an all too often mediocre art directs the mind's eye towards a wholly external type of majesty in which the inessential triumphs. Yet in God, all is interior and everything is essential. "Jesus Christ, without any assets and without any works appearing as science, is in his own order of sanctity. He never invented anything, he did not reign; but he was humble, patient, saint, saint to God, terrible to the demons and without any sin. Oh! But he did come in great pomp and in fabulous magnificence in the eyes of the heart that can see wisdom!"

There are on the portals of our cathedrals, some very beautiful Christs in majesty, but the simplest crucifix reveals better the majesty of God. Because it is in death that we can see—without any possible objection—the intensity and purity of love without which majesty is not absolutely majesty. Some mystics have been more sensitive to intensity, others to purity. Both are necessary to the same degree, and demand no other element. Humility goes with purity. Once I was tempted to prostrate myself before a woman whose whole life was one of devotion. Popular language expresses well the feelings I had: "One would kneel before such a woman!" She was neither a princess nor a queen, but how majestic she was in the extreme modesty of her demeanor, her stance, the way she held her head, her environment! Yet, it would have been enough for a hint of self-interest, an atom of selfishness or self-satisfaction, a shadow of calculation or intrigue to appear in her eyes and the majesty of humility would have disappeared from her brow and my feeling of veneration would have vanished. Indeed, a God without humility cannot be adored. One could not imagine such a ravage of the Majesty.

DISCRETION—God only has an absolute respect for the freedom of man. He created it, and it was not in order to petrify it or violate it, which is why he never calls out or imposes himself. He suggests, he proposes, he invites. He does not say: "I want," but: "If you want. . . ." Phrases such as "Commandments of God" and "Will of God" must be perceived and understood according to love. God does not reproach: he leaves this task to our conscience: "He is greater than our conscience" (1 Jn 3:20). He remains hidden so as not to be irresistible; his invisibility is modesty. He does not want us to prove him in such a way that our reason would be compelled. Indiscretion, which is incompatible with majesty, would mean an extension of self-love: exactly what we finally can perceive at the root of our imperialisms and clericalisms. But the voice of God is barely distinguishable from silence: it is a voice of fine silence. I cannot say timidity, since timidity is often growing off pride and prevents daring.

And God's daring is infinite: creation, incarnation. We must try to think, in our elusive moments of finest sensitivity, of the coexistence of contraries. We must try other words, but as if we were blushing at the risk. Perhaps chastity? Gregory Nazianzen, who was a poet, wrote boldly: "*Prima Virgo, sancta Trinitas* . . . the first Virgin was the Holy Trinity.*" I remember this when hearing Saint-John Perse praising Paul Valéry's incomparable chastity of language (as well as fidelity and modesty in the Latin meaning of the word). Of Valéry Larbaud, he said that "a secret modesty protected him equally from facileness and ostentation . . . from all narcissism as from all exhibitionism." And since I have decided not to give in to the suspicious fear of anthropomorphism, why should I hesitate to credit God with the qualifications of the great poets? In the same way, when I hear a character of Miguel del Castillo tell a companion: "Believe me, it is very difficult to give. I would like you to understand one thing: no matter what I give you or do for you, you owe me nothing. Do you hear me? Nothing.", I do not hesitate to believe that God talks to me in the same way. But my conscience wants to owe him, knowing that it would be a dishonor to fail to honor through gratitude the gratuitousness of God.

TENDERNESS—I shall speak prudently about the tenderness of God. What the word brings to mind is so beautiful that we would wish to transpose it as it is in the kingdom where all is effusiveness and nothing is dry. Yet one must criticize it without complacency. Tenderness often has automatic gestures, extending to the other or projecting on the other a spontaneous vibration which might well be nothing more than self-love. Delusion is rife here. The mystics denounced it, Fénelon more strongly and systematically than his peers, because he knew from experience that the dry and bitter peace is what accompanies centrifugal love with the least risk. Yet, one encounters towards God as towards creatures, purified tendernesses, regained after asceticism. Then nothing could be more deeply human, thus divine. I cannot refuse this to God. Jesus signifies this wonder to us, he whose gestures cannot be suspected of being automatic. He had nothing to purify; he was pure as God is pure. "What is good has been explained to you, man: this is what Yahweh asks of you: only this, to act justly, to love tenderly and to walk humbly with your God" (Mi 6:8).

At first I thought of calling this little book: *L'Enfance de Dieu* (The Childhood of God) in remembrance of the story of Claudel's conversion. During the vespers of Christmas 1886, at Notre Dame, he had "all of a sudden the heartbreaking feeling of innocence, of the eternal childhood of God, an ineffable revelation." I preferred to use *humility*, because God is also agony. Eternal childhood and eternal agony, which we distinguish but are not distinct in him, and one and the other, one in the other, are his very life. Regarding the admirable essay of Albert Béguin on Georges Bernanos,[29] I became convinced that it was possible for me to transpose in the immovable today of the Absolute this mystery which dazzled the novelist, of a childhood coming to the fulfillment of innocence only in the last throes of agony. Yet we know, especially since Freud, that the child is not innocent.

But even though he be somewhat of a polymorphous pervert, there is still enough innocence in him to symbolize innocence in the eyes of the adult who lost it. To say what man must be, Nietzsche prefers the image of the child to those of the camel and the lion. Not the child such as he is at birth, but such as is born of a double metamorphosis: that of the beast of burden responding to the weight of existence with a kneeling yes, of the predator responding to mud with a liberating no; and that of the ravishing animal in the child who pronounces the sacred yes, the only effective creator of new values. From the complex teaching of Zarathustra, I wish to remember here only this intuition: childhood is not at first a nostalgia, but a project; it is not the innocence of dawn, but the fullness of innocence to come. Yet it was not by chance that this image was chosen above others: it includes, while projecting it into the future, the nostalgia of the past; it retains the memory of a dawn which is itself devoid of memory.

The first innocence in this world has neither love nor freedom; the last innocence reaches, at the time of agony, the frontier of pure love and unrestrained freedom. For "there is no greater love than to give one's life for your friends" (Jn 15:13), and to be able to face death one must not be the slave of anything or anybody. But God is dawn shining and rising, while it is at the same time this weight of love that only the last agony can mean with a sufficiently severe approximation. The gravity of love at the borders of death is the matter of the "shining and rising" of the morning of God's freedom. In the West, the last imperfect expression of this harmony in which words and concepts break down, is given by Bach and Mozart: if their music is a poignant music of dawn, it is because the childlike beatitude it suggests embraces the entire universe of love's agonies.

In the look of a child there is a beam drilling into our adult conscience, arousing in us the remorse of never being what we should be. Innocence reveals us just as light brings out a relief. I would not say that if God did not exist, morality would have no foundation; but simply and without theory, that this look would be less implacable. Like the angel of Rilke, it is terrible.

But it would not be so terrible if it were not also absolutely disarmed. Its poverty and defenselessness make it barely possible for me to face it. Coming from very far, from a world without arms, without calculations, intrigues or lies—the world of the All-Other—it is also very near, sign of our "neighbor," poor and defenseless, towards whom our duty, right here and now, is to lay down all weapons of calculations, intrigue and lies.

Without misunderstanding what love is, one could not suspect God of after-thought or after-intention. Love does not surrender part of self while reserving the essential for itself: it surrenders the essential. Otherwise, it is not truly innocent. To hold back a thought or an intention while making sure it remains invisible means one wants to remain in control of self. Rousseau was not wrong in seeing in such a discordance created by after-thoughts between being and appearance, such a distance between the external mien and the heart's dispositions, the essence of original sin. Two centuries before Paul Valéry, he described the kingdom of after-thoughts as the place where all human debates take place. The Old Testament went to the root of all evil. If men are suspecting each other of not appearing to be what they are, it is because in Adam, their archetype, they first suspected God. Why does the Creator tell his creature that Life cannot be conquered as a prey but must be accepted as a gift? The most subtle of all beasts suggests the answer: he reserves to himself the right not to give it. Thus men cease to be innocent when they doubt the innocence of God.

If it were necessary for the purity of love to be unaware that one loves, one should say that God does not know his own essence. If it were impossible to know that one is humble without destroying humility, one should believe that God can only be humble in an absolute nescience of self. Indeed, one cannot know that one loves without loving to love, and this mars love. And how could one conceive of being transparent to self without ownership of self? And if humility is essential to love, how can one avoid that he who says: "I love," does not also say: "I am humble"? In human experience, one smiles and is led to dislike. When the *I* credits itself with such secondary qualities as physical strength or beauty, charm, even deftness in the handling of ideas, it is only ridiculous. But when the *I* makes a judgment of value and favor on the depth of itself, it is both ridiculous and hateful. Thus one could come to the conclusion that God is impossible unless one does not use experience as the starting point of an affirmation of the absolute Love, and declares mysteriously one in him—because it is revealed—that which implies a contradiction in us: namely that humility is lived in perfection and perfectly admired by itself as such. One would have good grounds in accusing me of invoking mystery just when I need its idea in order to fill a vacuum of idea in myself.

It is known that Malebranche accepted without revulsion a God loving himself with an egocentric love. He posited in him the logical priority of the perfection of being with regard to love: if God loves—he said—it is because he is perfect. He cannot not love himself, because it would be an imperfection not to love a perfect Self. This could not be accepted by Fénelon. For him, the logical priority belongs to love. If God is love it is because to love is perfection; love is the highest form of being; it is pure only if it excludes all trace—no matter how slight—of self-feeding. One must choose. If one thinks as Malebranche did, God is not humble. Then, what can one mean in affirming him to be perfect? If one prefers to follow Fénelon, God does not love himself. But the archbishop of Cambrai always guarded himself against such a daring—if not absurd— consequence. Are we going around in circles? I believe we would if God were not the Trinity.

The mystery which seems to complicate God, does in fact

simplify him. I mean by this that only the Trinity can affirm his simplicity—in the primitive meaning of absence of fold, folding on oneself, withdrawing into self. God is humble only if he is simple. He is simple only by plurality within unity.

There can be no narcissism—either in knowledge or in love—no curving up on self to complicate the being, if one is self only by tending towards the other, being motion towards the other. This is precisely in what we suffer at not being able to achieve it in human love, because we are ourselves before we love, and in love itself we remain ourselves independently of love. Though we do feel that love would be perfect if it were ourselves by making us part of one another while constituting our being: thus one would only be self by being outside of self. No one in this world remains totally alien to such a feeling, no matter how dehumanizing degradation can be. Even if such a feeling is very faint, it can be the starting point—thanks to Revelation, but without falling into fideist extrinsicism—of an adhesion to Trinity as mystery of simplicity, therefore of God's humility.

The innocent, in the Latin meaning of the word, is the one who does not harm either himself or others. When selfishness rules, one labors at hurting others so as not to harm oneself. But Jesus of Nazareth, who gives the conditions of the reign of love, teaches on the contrary that the measure in which we hurt the others is the measure in which we harm ourselves. Thus, he upsets the whole game. He is a nuisance, and he is killed. Nothing is easier and such is vileness itself, for harming the one who forbids to harm carries no risk. What happened to Jesus happens throughout history to all those who bear a reflection of eternal Innocence: they are annihilated. This, as we know, can be accomplished in many ways: violence or ruse or established disorder. If the Incarnation had been triumphant and glorious in the eyes of men, it would not have revealed the Innocent. The world would not have failed to integrate God into its order of harmfulness. In fact, it does continuously labor in order to make the churches forget of Whom they are the sacrament, and it quite often succeeds. Hence the present distrust towards them. Emmanuel Lévinas saw quite correctly that "the idea of a persecuted truth" is the "only possible modality of transcendence. Not [he pointed out] because of the moral quality of humility that I do not want to challenge in any way, but because of its *mode of being* which may be the source of its moral value. To manifest oneself as humble, allied to the vanquished, the poor, the persecuted; this is precisely a mark of not being in order. In this defeatism, in this timidity which dares no dare, this solicitation which is shy of soliciting and is non-daring in itself, in this solicitation of a homeless beggar who has nowhere to lay his head—left at the mercy of a *yes* or *no* of the one who takes in—the humiliated man is an absolute nuisance; he is not of the world. Humility and poverty are a way of being—an ontological (or meta-ontological) mode—and not a social condition. To appear in this poverty of an exile is to interrupt the coherence of the universe. To pierce through immanence without taking one's place in it."[30]

What the mystics call "passive state" can help us get a weak and remote glimpse of the eternal childhood of God, Eden of perfect simplicity. There is a pre-reflective passive state. Maine de Biran has analyzed it with subtlety as he perceived it in his adult consciousness. He evokes moments of blessed harmony with himself and with nature interrupting at times, too rarely and too briefly—for instance during a walk—the uneasiness and exhaustion to which he is accustomed. Unable to bring them on at will or to prolong them, he looks elsewhere for an antidote to his sadness: he scatters himself in society life, hoping to numb this unbearable feeling of vacuum. But entertainment does not go without remorse. While he is in the midst of the social whirlwind, solitude seems more attractively full and less bitter. However, as soon as he settles in it, he is attracted again by the outside agitation. Mood only is responsible for these variations that cannot be adequately explained by either the course of ideas or the dispositions of the will. It is without us and in spite of us that sadness and joy come and go as in a game.

We are affected by the changes in our body, we depend on our vital organism. There are purely affective states that are in me, do not come from me, and therefore are not me. But in the measure with which we refuse—since such a slavery is painful—to abandon ourselves to this passivity, the *I* comes forth as an activity. It does not matter here how Maine de Biran understands this coming forth: his philosophy of the "I want" interior to the "I think" drew many commentaries and discussions. What concerns here my limited purpose is this: the active and reflective life through which man finds himself and achieves himself partially by separating himself from what is not him, by opposing that of which he is not the source, creates in turn a new passivity, of a completely different nature, as luminous as the first one was dark; to a certain point it excludes effort and the consciousness of self is blurred, but without remorse and with joy. Another life begins, which the philosopher calls "life of the spirit" or "third life." The first one, which was affective, was marked by the absence of self, passivity with regard to sensible objects. The second one, which was human, was marked by the activity of the self in effort. The third one, going beyond effort, is a quiet abandonment, shall one say to God? Biran, who in the last years of his life was a constant reader of Pascal and Fénelon, will not say so before having first guarded himself against delusion. In any event, he perceived even if he did not experience, the passive state which can only be described by the mystics.

Passive state, state of childhood: God communicates to the soul his own Childhood, that is his very Life, totally stripped of self, all Innocence, Simplicity, Humility. In his commentaries on Maine de Biran, Gabriel Madiner does indeed direct his gaze towards this super-awareness of the deiform creature, therefore of God. "Through effort," he writes, "the being grasps himself only in relation to the body that he moves; he grasps himself only as power-to-move-self. To know oneself in effort, to say *I*, is to know oneself then in an imperfect and obscure way. . . . My *I* is not my *being*, it is the affirmation that only I can give to my being. . . . In the life of the spirit, the *I* gets blurred . . . How can the attainment of the being coincide with the disappearance of personal consciousness?

"It may be that there is a problem only because we consider the awareness of self as a summit which must be part of the most perfect mode of existence of which we can conceive, but if the awareness of *I* were only a limitation, if the *I* that we posit in this awareness which is human life, were only a way of opposing ourselves, of *distinguishing ourselves from that with which we cannot unite ourselves*, if the *I* were only the screen that hides us from ourselves, one could imagine a higher mode of being in which the self has lost the awareness of self, separate entity, though remains conscious of the being which it is. . . . To say *I*, to stand as *I*, this is less a grasp of self as being than as self separated from being."[31]

So that what makes man great—his power to reflect—also marks his limit. He will not go to God without giving up this limit which he holds very dear since it is his proper strength. He fears certainly above all a simplicity which does not say *I*. Which is why he imposes his own existence to the others. In God, there is nothing that could be imposed: nothing artificial. Thus no process in being and acting, nothing answering the question *how*. What Pierre Emmanuel says about the beatified poor of the Gospel, I can say *a fortiori* about God: "Its perfect detachment makes it so clear that this water knows nothing of its own limpidity." In the same vein, Bonhoeffer says: "Who has a pure heart? He who stains his heart neither with the evil he commits nor with the good he does."

The mystery of the Trinity is the essential of Christian faith. In order to insure ourselves against the suspicion of ideology, to guard against the temptation of the modern form of infantilism called impatience (what one does not understand immediately is held as being null and void, what cannot be immediately convertible into *praxis* has no interest), one must reflect as the Church did historically. The Church started her reflections with Jesus Christ, historical event. Who is this man? The apostles did not affirm their faith in his divinity before they had reached the term of a genesis. They first heard Jesus say "Father" to God by using a word—ABBA—which means filial abandonment at the very root of the being. They saw him act according to an equally immediate experience of God and man as if he had been at the same time God looking at man, and man looking at God.

They witnessed this unique intimacy lived, not only before them, but for them, because he invites them to share: "Say as I do: Abba, Father." The intimacy is maintained in extreme suffering when God is mute and the men cruel to excess: "Father, into your hands I deliver my spirit. . . . Forgive them." Resurrected, he shows that God *is-with* this man, but the question is: is this man God? Are God and Jesus two or one? On Pentecost Sunday, the apostles are overcome by the Spirit of Jesus. The experience of this infusion is such that they can only interpret it metaphorically. This is quite different from the poetic enthusiasm of the Greeks. They now have in themselves One whom Jesus had in himself. He leads them to the same acts, to facing the same risks, to the same courage in the face of death. It is indeed the Spirit of Jesus, but it is none other than the Spirit of God, since God alone can give the Spirit. "Already the spirit of man, our own spirit, that which no one can take away from us, that which, moreover, we are totally incapable of giving to anyone. Only God can give his Spirit, to be himself facing himself."[32]

Thus, Jesus is God. But he addresses God as "You." God talks to God. God says that he is the one sent by God. God's food is to do God's will. Therefore there is a duality in God. And the Spirit, being also God, is a Third person. The Church confronted with this paradox of God one and triune, understood very quickly that if it were not rigorously kept, human hope would be lost. "If the Incarnation," said Cyril of Jerusalem, "had been pure imagination, salvation too will be pure imagination." If God himself did not become man, how could man become God? And how could a unipersonal God become incarnate? As soon as the question is asked, it destroys itself: such a Man-God would have no other God than himself: he would be the worshiper of himself.

If the Church led a passionate combat during the first centuries of its history so that the depth of the mystery not be abolished for the benefit of an immediate rationality, it is because rigorous logic—expression of a superior rationality always demanded by the Holy Spirit in spite of our temptations to mediocre compromises—commanded it not to separate in the unity of its faith the triple belief in the Trinity, in the divinity of Jesus Christ, and in the divinization of mankind. If God were not Trinity, the Incarnation would be a myth, and our hope vanity. And one must guard against letting the horizon of this hope become too blurred, as happens only too often in certain catecheses. When the Church talks about salvation, it does not only say *of what* man is saved—namely sin and an inferior form of finitude—but *for what*, namely his participation in God's life.

If the promise of such a salvation is universal, it is inconceivable that Christianity, transmitting it from century to century, could ever be a gnosis. One often needs long and complex discourses and at times the use of knowledgeable systematizations, in order to convince the learned to interrupt the discourse and the erection of the system with the spirit of childhood, which is the only one compatible with the simplicity of God. Are they repelled by infantilism? One could not blame them, since they have good reasons for being cautious. In fact, Saint Paul warns us all: "Brothers, you are not to be childish in your outlook. You can be babies as far as wickedness is concerned but mentally you must be adult" (1 Cor 14:20). This intelligence, which has nothing to do with a clutter of concepts, coincides with the spirit of childhood in this: that it originates from a simple reflection on a common experience. The Trinitarian God is summoned by human love in its day to day reality. The Incarnation responds to such a concrete appeal.

In this world, love is a mingling of joy and suffering. Joy of telling the one you love: "You and I, we are not two but one." Suffering, since we are compelled to admit that when we say this, we tell not what is, but what we would want to be and cannot be. For if the lover and the beloved were not two any more, there would not be another one; and by the same token, love would cease to exist. What would be left would be self-love. But self-love is not love: it is complacency, neither welcome nor gift. Contrary to what certain Romantics imagined, love is not consummated in the absorption or fusion of two in one. The dream of Tristan and Isolde enchanted by the blessed disappearance of the "and" between their names, between their beings, into the Night, disappears itself tragically into Death. Love demands at the same time distinction and unity, otherness and identity. In the human condition the profound wish of being not only united with the other but *one-with* him while remaining self, is incoercible and unrealizable. Which is why no one enters the kingdom of love without suffering.

The mystery of the Trinity is the eternal fulfillment of this wish. Each one of the Three Persons is for himself only by being for the two others. The Father can only exist as Father distinct from the Son by giving all of himself to the Son; the Son can only exist as a Son distinct from the Father by being a total gift of love to the Father. The Father does not first exist as a person sufficient unto self and for self: it is the act of begetting the Son that makes him a person. One must thus avoid saying that the Father is "the One who" gives himself; rather he is "Act of" giving self. The same is true of the Son and Holy Spirit. What is thus revealed to us is that the relation of love is the original form of being. Or, to use other words: the core of the being is love, or communion. Every person can only be self outside of self. Their ecstasy is perfect in this: that the impossibility of withdrawal unto self is absolute. Any reflection about the Trinity that would leave the possibility of a God looking at himself (or an "incurvation," to use the word of Saint Bernard) would be tainted with error. God is in the mode of loving.

Why three Persons, and not two? Two approaches to the mystery of the Spirit can be proposed. The first one starts from the demand of reciprocity, essential to the perfection of love. In human love this reciprocity can only be perceived through signs: in itself it escapes the lovers. "I love you, and I see that you love me from the words you tell me, the gestures you make, the way you behave towards me. But I cannot see your love itself." Hence this suffering, and this temptation to doubt when these words and gestures and behavior seem less spontaneous or less ardent. Hence also this violent desire to know the love of the other in another way than through these signs, the presence of which enchants us but the decrease of which hurts us, and the absence of which leads us to despair. Saint Augustine wrote on this topic one of those sentences that memory loves and of which he was such a genius: "*Videt illa illum; videt ille illam; amorem nemo videt . . .* She sees him; he sees her; none sees love. . . ." In the Trinity, the Holy Spirit is Love itself: Love of the Father for the Son, Love of the Son for the Father. A mutual kiss. The reciprocity of hypostatized love. Another approach to this mystery can be attempted on the basis of the demand for purity which is also essential to the perfection of love. If there were no Third Person, the Father would find in the Son and the Son in the Father, a possession of self. The one would be for the other a projection, an extension of self. There could not be a total exclusion of ownership. If the reciprocal love of the Father and the Son opens up on a Third Person, there is no possession: poverty is absolute.

If God were not Trinity, he would not be Love in itself. Even if he were One, he would not be God. Of course, no Christian would dare talk about three gods. But we must beware of certain expressions that risk paving the way for dangerous fixations of the imagination. A few days before his death, abbé Jules Monchanin wrote: "Please, let people stop using the expression 'divine family' that the Fathers of the IVth Century would have anathematized. The discovery of the full personality of each person as a basis for all forms of spirituality, especially that of the Christian homes, is one of the graces of our times, but this discovery must not becloud the infrangible unity of the divine essence. That would be falling back into paganism." Grafted on the Gospel, theology must return to the Gospel. The words of Jesus, in their very humility, have then an incredible wealth of resonance: "The Father and I are one" (Jn 10:30). "That they may be one, as we are one" (Jn 17:22). "The Holy Spirit that the Father will send in my name, will teach you everything" (Jn 14:26). The trinitarian mystery sheds light on all the paths of human existence. One must "imitate God," as Saint Paul said (Ep 5:1). Be it in our most private personal life or in the exercise of our freedom at the different levels of family, work, the State or international society, it all amounts to this: not to be deluded about what love is. The vocation of man, the meaning of his life therefore, is to live as God lives, thus to love as he loves. Nothing could tear such a desire from his heart.

Because God is transcendent, he is immanent to the created being. Reason, getting rid of the phantasm of spatial exteriority, can only understand transcendence as a beyond in interiority: God is in me more me than me. But the trinitarian mystery reveals, if I dare say so, a higher transcendence which is a deeper immanence. God is present to himself only in the mode of being present to the other. His relation to self is his relation to the other. He can only grasp himself in and through the communication of self to the other. He is not the *Being* who effaces himself as if he had to overcome dialectically an autarchic Substance: he is the *Act of* effacing himself. If the concept of humility implies the negation of a proud relation to one's self, one must negate the negation in order to attribute it to God. If stripping supposes a possession of self logically anterior to the act of abandoning it, one must deny the logical anteriority when one talks about God. The essence of God is to be infinitely distant from self. He is near to the other only. Super-transcendence of intimacy, thus intimacy beyond immanence. Were God less distant from himself, he would be less intimate with me.

If man were not attached to self as a singular being, separated from all the others, he could not say *I*. The secession of the consciousnesses is a constituent of their subjectivity. In itself, it is not an evil, but evil takes root in it. For to be as a self inclines one to prefer oneself, to love less, and finally not to love at all what is other than self. How much more deeply if for God, of whom man is the image, "I is another." The Christian concept of original sin cannot be clarified in the relation between relative and absolute, finite and infinite, or beings and Being. The Trinity is the Abyss that has no common measure with the ontological abyss. Sin, in the eyes of faith, is also without a common measure with fault or even radical evil such as the philosophers understand it on their own plane.

In the last pages of *le Rêve* (The Dream) Zola shows us Angélique, a State-raised girl, giving her school report to her fiancé, the very rich and very noble Félicien de Hautecoeur. "Now she was," says Zola, "in a state of perfect humility, she wanted him to know quite well from what depths he had pulled her out to raise her to the glory of his legendary name and his great wealth. These were her sheepskins, this administrative piece of paper, this release showing a date and a number. She leafed through it once again, then gave it to him without any confusion, in the joy of knowing that she was nothing and that he made her everything. "Reading such an admirable page directs my eyes towards the humility of welcome in God-Trinity. Here there is neither rich nor poor: the rich does not enrich the poor, but there is a consubstantiality of welcoming poverty. The Father, though he is called Principle, is Father only through the Son; the Son is Son only through the Father; the Spirit is Spirit only through the Father and the Son. Each one of the Persons would be nothing if the Others were not making him All. Accepting is giving; giving is accepting. There is no possession anywhere. Therefore man runs no risk of being made into a property of God. Since God does not possess himself, how could he possess us?

Rimbaud affirms: "I is another." How can it be that "wood finds itself being a violin?", that "brass wakes up as a bugle?", that this eighteen year old adolescent is a poet? "This is not his fault." "I watch the blossoming of my thought: I look, I listen: I swing my bow: symphony moves in the depths or jumps up to the stage." Inspiration finds its source elsewhere. A poet is poet only through another. "So many *selfish* people [underlined in the text] claim to be authors . . . their intelligence is . . . one-eyed." The fault lies in having the soul of an owner. One must not write for himself alone: one must find a language which is "soul for soul." These lines from *Lettres du Voyant*[33] (Letters from the Seer) are at the extreme opposite of aestheticism. What is "given" is not for pleasure. What does not come from self is not for self. Rimbaud does not name the other who is his I. If he is a mystic, he is so "in the raw stage." But whether one be "raw" or not, a mystic is always one who undertakes to be self only through another, therefore for the others. The Trinity is the super-transcendent model of this *through* and this *for*, that—under the name of charity—are the key to any human progress.

At the level of created beings, the expression "to be through others" is dangerously ambiguous. If one does not understand it to mean—rigorously so—lack of ownership of self or reception within the orb of love, it runs the risk of evoking what Zundel calls our "prefabricated being," or as others say: our archeology or prehistory, meaning what came before the birth of our freedom. To praise as supreme ideal this "being-through-others" would be a dangerous misconception. For "we are called to liberty" (Gal 5:13) and our vocation is to be born to ourselves. I am borrowing from Father Edouard Pousset three definitions which will clarify the matter.

Universal—This is the element in which everything communicates and, in each one of us, it is that through which he communicates with the others. Every man is potentially universal, in his desire, then by his capability of knowing and sharing. What is universal overcomes all limitations through the power of negating what is particular and of impelling everyone, beyond himself, into this element of communication between all. One who has a vocation to the universal is thus himself only insofar as he gives himself up.

Particular—That which is defined in itself by a principle remaining exterior to it. Thus, being a member of the French community, I am what I am because of family traits, ethnic background, geographical, social, historical influences . . . in short, I am what others made me. This definition by others and by exterior circumstances—let us say this making of myself by others—is not all that I am, but it is all of me under an essential aspect: the aspect of my being-through-others. Thus I have to accept being defined by affiliation, sex, biological roots sentencing me to death. . . . I did not choose, I was not consulted. Such is reality. My freedom can start only from this acceptance.

Singular—The subject wants to act . . . He has the power to implement his own universality, to deny his particularity and adapt it to communion with others. As a singular subject, I have to discover my particularity and act so that it will not become the limit that stops me, but the means through which I can communicate with others in going beyond myself. This is possible for a singular subject because he is not only a particular being limited by an exterior principle of negation, but is precisely a subject, namely one who has the power to negate. I am thus, at the same time, determined—as a particular being—and determining.[34]

Rereading *le Narcisse* (Narcissus) by Paul Valéry, I find some lines describing admirably what God is not, and one could at the extreme limit conceive of a hypostatized Incurvation on self:

. . . the one who approaches himself . . .
To the enfolding of self into love . . .
What a loss in self . . .
Captive of the monster of self-love . . .
Until this charming moment I did not know myself
Not knowing how to cherish and reach myself!

But I, beloved Narcissus,
care only for my own essence;
Anyone else's heart is mystery to me
Anyone else is absence. . . .
The most beautiful of mortals can only love self.
I love! . . I love! . .
and who could love anyone but himself!

It is the poem of the Self who is nothing but Self and is delighted in self. Who will compose the song of the Being immeasurably distant of self, the one who has no mirror to look at his own Face and love it? Such a poet would exalt the joy of the Image, that is not similar to self as Same but as Other; the happiness there is in not being able to approach self or in living in no other way than by dying of an eternal death which, far from annihilating the being, builds it up. No smooth waters, no sheet of water, no slumbering universe but as in Saint John: breath, stream, living water, flame, fire.

Gide has also certain confessions showing the way to a Vacuum robed in prestige. In *Les Faux-Monnayeurs* (The Counterfeiters): "The new notebook in which I write these lines, will not be soon out of my pocket. It is a mirror I carry along with me. Nothing happening to me has a real life to me until I can see myself reflected in it." and in *Si le grain ne meurt* (Unless a grain dies): "In the mirror of the small writing-desk . . . that my mother had put in my room and on which I used to work, I would watch my features, unceasingly; I studied them as an actor would have done, I would search my lips, my eyes, for the expression of all the passions I wished to feel . . . In those days I could not write—and I was almost going to say: think—except in front of that small mirror. To grasp my emotions, my thoughts, it seemed to me that I had first to read them. Like Narcissus, I was looking into my own image; all the sentences I would then write have remained somewhat bent."

By cheapening the vocabulary of love, Christianity is easily watered down. When I meet young men and young girls irritated by such an inflation of words, I am not shocked. Quite the opposite! It means that either by my words I participate in spite of myself in this cheapening or that they sense in their parents, teachers or friends what can be not only shallow or sentimental in love, but I would even say: positively dangerous. Indeed, there is a concept and a practice of love remaining, even in adulthood, stubbornly adolescent. This is already degraded childhood and it is not yet agony. It can be sensed that it will never reach the latter stage, except perhaps at the very moment of death. This is love as a vital instinct, juvenile claim for the irrational as such, justification of unreasonable or premature commitments, shallow militancy, forgetfulness of the necessary centerings and mediations, systematic anti-institutionalism, infantilism of thought, romanticism of action. Some people say: Love, love . . . , as others: Spirit, spirit, or: Lord, Lord. . . .

I hope to bring some clarity on what I call paradoxically the Agony constituting the Being and the Life of God, through what I am going to say about the creative Act. It is nothing else but absolute seriousness of love, stripped mercilessly of any arbitrary feature, amateurishness or game, and seen at the end of its endlessness or futureless future. Bernanos is very much in my mind, he whose painful way had led me to meditate on the eternal encounter of childhood and agony. Remembering him prevents me from having to face the terrible reproach— justified or not—that Lévinas directed once at Heidegger [who] "had brought down pathetic thoughts to the level of professorial categories."[35] Bernanos helps me to keep experience and reflection tightly knit in all things. I say: *agony* because *death* would be too violent a paradox. And yet! Talking about God, we are beyond antinomies. Why, at the moment of Jesus' death, should I cease hearing him telling me: "Who has seen me has seen the Father"? It is an homage to the beloved when the lover forgets for her sake to eat, sleep, rest and even to breathe or live. But the limit must not be an object. Especially when it comes to creation which is efflorescence, effusion, overbrimming Life!

God is absolutely self-sufficient. It is necessary to affirm it not so much because—from the viewpoint of reason—there would be a contradiction in the notion of an insufficient Infinite, but in order to safeguard—from the viewpoint of faith—the gratuitousness of the creative Act. If there is in God something lacking or a need impelling him to create, all we have said about the inviolable purity of love will collapse. One could multiply distinctions between God such as he is in himself and God such as he acts "outside"; nothing could change the matter and the game of explanations will carry the risk of hiding the perfect simplicity of his being. In any event, we would be ascribing an interested motivation to God, we would lock him into self; at a deeper level, we would be hurting the simplicity of love. If God is dependent, as we have said and will say again, it has to be in a way which changes nothing of his self-sufficiency.

Then one must guard against the crudest of delusions: that of a spatial and temporal exteriority of the creative Act. God did not decide to create at a given moment of his existence: his existence has no moments. When Saint Irenaeus talks about a "Council" of the three Persons of the Trinity establishing an "economy" of creation, he is not deceived by the anthropomorphism of the imagery; neither is Saint Ignatius of Loyola when he contemplates the divine Persons deciding the Incarnation. Creative initiative is coexistent with the eternity of God which has no temporal extension. The same obtains from the historical viewpoint: to locate creation at the beginning of time, to look at it as an event of the past, as a "push" through which the world started to exist is really nonsensical. Equally nonsensical is the idea of God the craftsman. Manufacturing or producing implies an operative process incompatible with the simplicity of God. From the viewpoint of faith, such an absurdity turns into a scandal since it is beneath love to make a ready-made thing. Love cannot not want to let what it creates create itself by itself. It is a genuine contagion of existence. I am wary of the phrase "to make." I cannot say it without thinking "to manufacture" or "to produce." I prefer to say that in creating God "does" nothing, "makes" nothing, but that he exists "in a contagious manner."

Such are the true teachers. There was a Religious by my side for more than twenty years; he never gave me an order, he never even gave me a formal piece of advice. Yet, his presence was a constant call to a higher existence. And there are men and women who, by looking with friendship at teenagers who have not been properly loved and are on their way to becoming members of this quasi-vacuum of life called gangland, succeed in turning them back to the greatness of life. One needs a great deal of humility. God is not a Star appointing satellites to himself. It remains true, as has often been said since Hegel, that for a subject, to be is a manifestation. The original meaning of the Greek word *aletheia* pleads in favor of such a concept of reality as non-hiding (privative alpha and *lanthano*). It prevents us from imagining the self-sufficient fullness of God as a circle in which the trinitarian love would be locked. If it is part of the essence of the being to unveil itself, God unveils himself excessively, going beyond his self-sufficiency. Excess is an open self-sufficiency.

Such a clash of words will not surprise people who have had the experience of a necessary expansion of love beyond the borders of a perfectly united family. Necessary? Such a necessity is freedom itself: nothing and no one are putting pressure here. What remains irreducibly mysterious and therefore impossible to conceive in the creative Act, is the link between the perfect completion of God in himself and the eternal project—interior to this very completion—of opening self to others. One can however perceive that if God is Love, his complete perfection is not an enclosure but an initiative.

The word *manifestation* is, after all, a fallacy. It easily brings to mind the idea of a show. God is not looking at himself; he does not make a show of himself to his creation; neither nature nor man is a spectacle to him. There is always some pride in a show. It would be best to talk about creative humility: God effaces himself by renouncing to be everything. Such a renunciation is his very being, and in no way an episode. It is his All-Power in an act of self-effacement and not of show. A show would be a confession of deficient power. Self-effacement is, on the contrary, supreme power.

Thus, I will not say that God limits his power in order to make room for freedoms other than his own. I prefer to say that he exerts it with excess (in the precise meaning of the word). It is the All-Power of an absolute renunciation of self which makes God a triune being—each Person being self only *through* and *for* others—and which creates freedoms. Thanks to this humility, creatures can be in themselves and by themselves. Rigorously speaking, God gives them to themselves, which means that he gives himself totally by wanting them to be other and not simply an extension of himself. There is no pretense: God's Power does not play games. The biblical and dogmatic affirmation of creation is the opposite of any form of pantheism and emanationism in which, the creature not being really other than God, its unity with him would not be, could not be, the unity of love. Love, with one and the same gesture, differentiates and unifies. Thus God can at the same time be himself and other than self. He can constitute the other as his proper reality. Such a mystery is not an enigma: experience can help us get an inkling of it. To love is, at the same time, to respect the other and unite oneself with him. To respect him means to want him to be—really be in himself—other than self; this is the heart of justice.

To unite oneself with him means to want that, remaining other, he become more-me-than-me, namely that he never be treated as just one who is totally other. There is in any love, even a very imperfect one, a simultaneous affirmation and negation of others. The negation does not cancel the affirmation; the other does not cease to be other in the act through which I call him or make him mine. It is difficult for us to think about these two concepts—respect and union, justice and love—as being interior to one another. In God there is the very Act of his Simplicity. The trinity is the eternal unity of an eternal differentiation. Thus Christ is, when God creates, the one who is indivisibly wanted as other and denied as being other. He is the perfect unity in otherness, the very achievement of creative love; the Man-God. Thus there is no such thing as creation first and then incarnation, even though there was a genesis and a historical appearance of Christ. In other words, the creative Act has a Christic structure. "Before the world was made, he chose us, chose us in Christ," says Saint Paul (Ep 1:4). "He is the image of the unseen God, the first born of all creation. . . . Before anything was created, he existed and he holds all things in unity" (Col 1:15-17).

Yet, Christ is crucified. Here we see the vulnerability of God and what we dared call his eternal "agony." Love does not manipulate the freedoms it creates. It cannot compel them to love. In letting them create themselves, God accepts the risk of seeing them turn away or turn against him. A love that creates freedoms can only be a suffering love. Gregory the Thaumaturge is not afraid of talking of the "passion" of the impassive God. And before him, Saint Irenaeus saw the Word of God impressed as a cross (*kechiasmenos* translates in the Greek retroversion, the Latin *infixus*) on the whole creation.

This is why, he says essentially, this very Word was visibly hung on the wood of the cross.[36] On this cross, says Evdokimov,[37] "God, against God, took the side of man." In this he shows himself as God since love cannot refuse to go to the very limit of itself. It is sacrificial, otherwise it would be limited. But man remains free before the cross. And God's respect for man's freedom also goes the limit of itself. The divine sacrifice can be a failure. Man's refusal is possible: thus his misery, thus the agony of his Father in the most secret depth of himself.

The intelligence of the faith must be careful not to separate what is distinguished by representation and what is proposed to our reflection as dogmatic precisions by the Church. When they are "atomized" and, as it were, lined up one behind the other, these precisions lose all credibility. Their coherence is fragile, and one doubts their originality. This cannot be avoided when reflection is not nourished by experience or when experience is not enlightened by reflection. In fact, experience, reflection and Christian dogmas together lead to the mystery of God in whom all is one: love, freedom, Trinity, creation, incarnation, cross of Christ, divinization of men, and even their possible damnation.

Hope is not unknown to God. God and I together hope in my salvation. Can we free divine hope from the temporality that such a concept seems to necessarily entail? Probably not altogether. But I prefer such an anthropomorphism which I can control, to another type which would take out of history this element of uncertainty that God introduced when he created man as a free being. God must not be rationalized. He is a beating heart. If, under the excuse of safeguarding his omniscience, I deny him hope, I petrify his eternity. A petrified eternity would be like a leaden sky over my head. And while singing "Love . . . love," I would simply go back to the *Eimarmene* or *Fatum* of the Ancients.

A man who had suffered all his life told God before he

died: "My God, if you exist, I forgive you." Letting my imagination go wild, I like to envision God hearing this prayer (for this is a prayer). He smiles gravely, without irony. He seriously welcomes the forgiveness of the man. He remembers that he had hesitated to undergo the risk of human suffering and of the "slaying" of the Lamb (Rv 13:8). He humbly opens his arms to greet his suffering and peaceful son. Anthropomorphism to be sure, but kept under control while I reflect upon it, taking care to touch this mystery of suffering with the hands of a nurse. For I know that when a man is suffering, he wants at the same time a religious explanation of his pain and he rejects what is going to be poured on his wound as an acid, knowing it ahead of time! He dreads the latter more than he hopes for the former.

All I can say is that for me, such as I am, nothing is less abstract than this: God is not the craftsman of the world. He did not make it the way a watchmaker makes a clock. He does not build ready-made stuff. On the contrary, he draws back so that the beings he calls forth can emerge by themselves and for themselves. They cannot come into being except through this "formless void" described in Genesis (1:2): emptiness, vagueness, pure multiplicity, pure exteriority, pure dispersion. Were God to intervene so as to avoid groping and disorders, resisting inertia, tidal waves, epidemics, the world would be for him nothing but an object to manipulate. Our imagination, slipping into infantilism, would probably see in this a greater love. But God does not love in the way we would want him to when we project our dreams onto him. He would spare us suffering only at the price of a paternalism through which he would cease being Love.

God is serious with regard to respect and suffering. We cannot come to either one of these two xxcept from a very great distance, and by leaning on our highest experience. In truth, God respects us too much to magically spare us suffering, and he respects himself too much to spare himself the suffering of our suffering. And when it comes to the evil brought forth by our freedom—violence, the "state of war" of which Lévinas says that it "suspends morality"—how much more demanding at this level the respect and how much deeper the suffering of creative Love! We are here at the heart of the mystery—I say it clearly: mystery—of God's humility.

Proust wrote about Wagner: "In him, no matter how sad the poet, he is consoled, overcome—that is to say unfortunately slightly cheapened—by the joy of the manufacturer." And Julien Green, admiring the Overture of *Die Meistersinger*: "This is genius with its marvelous assurance, I was going to say: his insolence." Knowing Wagner, the truth of these comments helps me to purify the idea I have of creation.

The "sadness" of God, of which the sadness of Jesus at Gethsemane is a sign, is not such that the joy of a manufacturer could console it or overcome it. "Insolence" goes very well with "manufacturer" and the two words together express very well what God is not: joy to be self, powerful, domineering, imposing oneself. The joy of God, a word translated from *agalliasis* which Saint Luke loves, is as humble as it is immense. It is the Other, and only the Other, who pours it into his renounced being. Each one of the Persons of the Trinity is the joy of the other, and man is the joy of God. It is impossible to manufacture without being self-complacent. Since God does not manufacture human freedom, human freedom can wound his heart and the joyful Act of creation is under the shadow of the cross. Wagner, powerful genius that he was, knew himself and wanted himself to be invulnerable: thus his "insolence." In this, he turned his back to God.

The word *kenosis*, which is still barbaric for many, is beginning to be known and used elsewhere than in the schools of theology and exegesis. It comes from the Greek *kenos*, empty, or *kenoo*, to empty. Saint Paul introduced in his epistle to the

Philippians (2:6-11) a Christian hymn, probably older than the epistle itself, in which the subject of this verb is Christ himself. This is the major reference: "His state was divine, yet he did not cling to his equality with God but emptied himself to assume the condition of a slave. And being as all men are, he was humbler yet, even to accepting death, death on a cross."

The experts have not yet stopped arguing about the theological impact of *ekenosen* in this text. It does seem that for the first Christians, probably not much concerned with metaphysics, who composed the hymn, the issue was not an eternal act of the Word, but simply the condition of poverty and humility chosen by Jesus in his terrestrial life. This is what Father Benoit stresses in a note in the Jerusalem Bible: "This concerns less," he says, "the fact of the Incarnation than its mode. Christ made man freely stripped himself not of divine nature, but of the glory it brought him by right, that he had in his pre-existence (cf. Jn 17:5) and which should normally have marked his humanity (cf. Mt 17:1-8)." Through his death on the cross Christ truly "annihilated," "emptied" himself of self: such is, in the eyes of some exegetes, the point of the text.

But Tradition allows us to enlarge, within the framework of all the Christian mysteries, the meaning of the word *kenosis*. In spite of secondary nuances, there is a deep agreement obvious during the first centuries between the Fathers of the East and the West, and nowadays between the Orthodox Sergei Bulgakov and the Catholic Hans Urs von Balthasar, which encourages us to place the *kenosis* in God himself and to discover in it the secret of his work and his being. Up to now, I have avoided the esoteric word, and I have said: *humility*, but *kenosis* was at the back of my mind. For me the two words were superimposed. I even had a flashing thought of calling this book *The Kenosis of the Father*. Never ceasing to hear the words of Jesus: "who has seen me has seen the Father," without which daring to talk about God would only be presumption, we have followed, in the words of René Char, "the stone path that his heart had made for himself," and it led us to the cross, supreme revelation of Glory.

The heart of my faith is that the *being* of God corresponds to his *appearing* in Christ. Jesus does not tell us only how man must love, but also and first how God loves. If there is a *kenosis* of Christ, it is because God, Father, Son, Holy Spirit, is eternally in *kenosis*, namely in an act of sacrificial offering of self. There is no need to be a Christian in order to know that no one enters the joy of loving without entering at the same time the suffering of loving. But the Christian establishes in God himself this reciprocity, I was going to say: this identity. God is what he becomes in Christ. There would be no *kenosis* of the incarnate Word if the Trinity—and not only the Word—were not in itself Power and Act of *kenosis*, which does not mean that the Father or the Spirit could have become incarnate. Tradition before Saint Augustine never thought of such a possibility. The temporality of Jesus' existence translates the proper form of the existence of the Word, different from that of the Father and the Spirit.

If the characteristic of love is to differentiate as much as to unite, there is no reason to be surprised that the difference between the three Persons is so great that only a very loose analogy enables us to apply to each one the concept of person in the same way.[38] The form of existence of the Son is to be Image, therefore pole of acceptance, humility and poverty in the Trinity. "He is not the *One* whom he expresses, namely the Father," but he is "what he expresses, namely God."[39] He is in *kenosis* as Image of the Father, but it is of a *kenosis* that he is the image. He would not be in *kenosis* if the Father were not in it. Bulgakov speaks of "a metaphysical and eternal Golgotha" of which the "historical Golgotha" would be the phenomenal translation. So be it! And such words are good if they catch our memory. But, let us make sure that the experience of love, such as we humbly live it, never ceases to be close to us in order to convince us that happiness and sacrifice, far from being mutually exclusive, are tied together! Otherwise, the idea of a celestial Golgotha is a scandal for the reason and a repulsive thing for the heart.

We are made in God's image, and our vocation is to be like him. When distractions remove us too far from ourselves, we approve of the demand of death which is in the heart of love, and we understand a little that God, who lives it in himself, wants it also for us. Jesus brings it to us in very simple words and very humble gestures. At certain times of lesser selfishness, when we are less afraid of being men, we allow him to tear off our masks—the masks we have made ourselves so as to become mediocre and not to have to die. Then we look, with naked faces, at the greatness of our freedom. And we ourselves claim what Jesus told us. His voice and ours become one: You are worth more than you think, your nobility is beyond the awareness you have of it in your scattered life. And here is an echo in the words of Bernanos:

> I think about him, and it is I that I discover little by little, as another himself, at the bottom of the mud pit in which I am still stirring.
>
> It is not a matter of conforming our will to his, because his will is ours, and even when we rebel against it, it is at the cost of tearing apart our inner being, monstrously scattering ourselves. Our will is united to his since the beginning of the world. He created the world together with us. . . . How sweet it is to think that, even when we offend him, we never cease completely to desire what he desires, in the very depths of the sanctuary of the soul! We really want what he wants, we truly want, without knowing it, our pains, our sufferings, our solitude, while we imagine that we only want our pleasures. We imagine

that we fear our death and run away from it, while we really want this death as he wanted his. Just as he sacrifices himself on each altar where Mass is offered, he starts dying again in each man going through death agony. . . . We want all that he wants, but we do not know that we want it, we do not know ourselves, sin makes us live at the surface of ourselves, we will not go back into ourselves until we die, and it is there that he waits for us.[40]

When childhood and agony coincide, we know ourselves and we know God. This, as much as it is possible, in the heart of life and action, in the full health of soul and body.

By linking together two words which have the same root: liberty and liberality, I think that I can point to the unfathomable depth of God. I am wary of Hegel since he conceived death—which he saw quite well as interior to God—as a dialectical necessity and not as a free spontaneity of love. God is not Necessity, he is Gratuitousness. If the word "decision" could be detached from the temporality it implies, to wit: if it were possible to think of a decision not as an act of the mind located at a given moment of time, but as an eternal act qualifying in its depth the being who makes it, one should say that God is a decision of absolute liberality. That is to say: liberal liberty. We could thus avoid degrading—by giving in to the pressure of imagination—love itself into a necessity: God loves, such is the way he is, he cannot be otherwise, he has no merit! People do say such things. They must not be accused too fast of being infantile. They mean that God is imagined as feeling the weight of love with the same necessity he would feel the weight of hatred if his nature were to hate. At the limit one equates divine love with an irresistible biological force. I will not say that beyond love there is freedom comparable, says Berdyaev, to a "bottomless well." The image seems to suggest that an abyss of darkness is logically preceding the appearance of God as decision to love. I rather tend to think that the decision to love, that is God himself, is the depth or rather the primordial non-depth. The ultimate secret where darkness is light. Liberty is liberality.

Ordinarily people reason as follows: suffering and happiness are incompatible; it is impossible that happiness not be essential to perfection; yet God is perfect, thus he is happy; if he is happy, he does not suffer; a God who suffers is not God. The witness of religious awareness is compatible here with logic: for the one as for the other the notion of a suffering of God is a stumbling block. If we were only dealing with logic, it would be possible to make it step back by convincing it that it is more rigid than rigorous and based only on a simplistic psychology. This is not too difficult and I shall endeavor to do it. But not to hurt spontaneous awareness is a more delicate task which has to be undertaken prudently. This is why it is important to appease it by affirming at the outset and without reservations, that God is happy with an absolute happiness. Nothing can darken the mystery of his Joy. But this very Joy is a mystery: not only higher and more total than ours, but different, totally different. However, it is our experience that invites us to refuse the dilemma: either God is imperfect and he suffers or he is perfect and he does not suffer. But what experience? Certainly not the crude experience in which feelings of pleasure and pain cannot coexist. A toothache cannot at the same time hurt us and give us pleasure. But as soon as we rise to other levels of sensitivity, the words "pleasure" and "pain" do not have the same meaning. Pain remains, because our vocabulary is poor, but not pleasure; it is rejected in favor of joy or happiness, depending on the case. And already there is something beyond sensations, towards finer affective states in which joy and pain are not so incompatible, even if one has not yet entered the kingdom of love.

The analytical genius of Marcel Proust, for one, can very well unravel this knot by shedding light on its complexity.

Aesthetics enjoys these borders of consciousness that ancient psychology ignored but that modern psychology, being better equipped, can explore. However, it is only at the level of freely accepted sacrifice for love that one can experience the paradoxical unity of suffering and joy. When one is not centered on self, when the other is the one to whom we say without lying too much, "You are all to me," when life or part of it is consecrated to others, suffering can be lived as essential to joy. It is perceived in this very simple little sentence, often expressed, of a friend who does a costly favor to a friend: "I am so happy to do this for you!" If we extend this, we can understand how the limit can be reached: the joy of dying of love. Suffering is not any more an imperfection or obstacle to happiness: it is happiness itself. The experience of artists—at least those who do not seek art for its own sake—can guide our sight. That of the mystics extends it by radically transposing it. God is the horizon and the beyond of the horizon.

Anthropomorphism? Yes, in any event. But I prefer this one to a contrary anthropomorphism which accepts an impassible God rationalized by dint of crediting him with intelligence and denying him a heart. The biblical God has entrails. He is a mother, as Isaiah said: "Does a woman forget the baby at the breast, or fail to cherish the son of her womb? Yet even if these forget, I will never forget you" (Is 49:15). A mother who would dare say she is so happy that the suffering of her children does not touch her, would be enjoying a monstrous happiness! A Father who, from the throne of his glory, would contemplate without pain what is happening at Gethsemane and at Calvary: who could call him Father? If an uncontrolled anthropomorphism can be dangerous, how much more a mixture of anthropomorphisms depending on the mood or the semblance of reason! Here, for instance: one keeps, if not the throne, at least the celestial observatory, and God is denied tears.

If the Church, in the IIIrd century, condemned the Patripassianists it was because their affirmation of a "suffering of the Father" was linked to a false conception of the Incarnation. We must not renew their error, but pry out of it the kernel of truth it contained, probably without their knowing it. It is enough in the following text of Charles du Bos, to give the word *detachment* its strongest meaning, with all its echoes of suffering and even death, in order to perceive something of these states of very fine sensitivity from which one rises more easily to an experience of God:

"It seems that there is in Saint Augustine a supreme refinement impelling him to perfect and, as it were, to caress with his words the things of which he must detach himself at the very moment he is going to become detached of them. The circle in which he moves is always the widest possible circle so that none of the motions seem to be cramped, or even take on the least appearance of antinomy. Detachment itself is in him a motion as graceful as a floral motion. This is because his soul is filled at the same time with fervor and ingenuousness, and when it leaves an object for one which is higher, it feels with a sure instinct that it will find in the higher object the best and the essence of the other, with always something *more*—a *more* coming from the new object and from his own new state. This certainty of an increase without real break gives to all the gestures of St. Augustine—and no less to his detachment—the easiest nobility. St. Augustine detaches himself from flowers with a feeling similar to the one with which Parsifal discovers them on the meadow."[41] "In life at its highest degree of intensity," said Cabasilas, "death and life are not opposed anymore, but they are entwined in the liberating figure of the Cross."

In *Le Soulier de Satin* (The Satin Slipper), when Prouheze starts on her course to adultery, the Angel tells her: "And I, I am coming with you." The Angel, here, is the sign of God.

What he tells the young woman, he tells all his children, unceasingly: it is the word of love in an act of redemption. Accompanying us in the depth, discreetly, almost silently. One word only, so that his presence be known at the time of the most acute attention. When we realize that he is there, we worship that which makes it so that he must be there, and which is himself. He could not come with us without entering in agony. Otherwise he would be indifferent to our misery. Then perhaps blasphemy would be permitted: he might as well be absent!

Two months before his death, Paul Valéry was also contemplating an Angel, another sign of God. But of a very different God. Spirit of pure intelligence, the evil of the world is asking him a question that will eternally remain a question. Ancient Narcissus has deserted the mythological universe and has become a metaphysical Angel. He looks at himself in the fountain and sees a weeping Man. His image is not to his image. Incomprehensible infidelity! His "marvelously pure spiritual substance" is "in the naked water this infinitely sad prey." "There was a sadness in the shape of Man that did not find its cause in the clear sky." "O my EVIL," it said, "what are you to me?" "He tried to smile to himself: he was weeping to himself." Enigma for God.

The Angel does not suffer, "for what causes pain in our unreliable natures only raises a question in the absolute essence." A question which wounds the universality and unity of knowledge, holds in abeyance its infallible operation but does not affect the luminous subject. "Who then is this one who loves himself so much that he is tormenting himself?", he said "I understand all things, and yet I see that I suffer." Two *Is*: the Angel and his image in the shape of Man, his incomprehensibly different twin. Not only different, but contrary. The Angel sees, the Man suffers. "This face is surely my face, these tears, my tears . . . and yet, am I not this power of transparency of which this face and these tears, and their cause, and that which would destroy this cause, are only imperceptible grains of duration?"

However, harmony is perfect in the heaven of ideas: they sparkle "in the light of each other, like the jewels they are in the crown of unitive knowledge." Why these tears and where from? "For I am pure," he said, "and Intelligence consuming effortlessly any created thing, while none can affect or change it, cannot recognize itself in this weeping face, in these eyes the light of which is softened by the moist imminence of tears. . . . O my surprise . . . Charming and sad head, is there then something other than light?" The surprise of God will have neither pause nor end. Man, because he weeps, makes Intelligence unintelligible to itself. "And for an eternity, he never stopped to know and not to understand."

Angel of Rilke, angel of Claudel, angel of Valéry: every one chooses his angel, the idea he has of God. I am not sure that the Angel of Valéry means to him the emptiness of heaven, the radical impossibility of God due to the evil of Man. I do not know either whether the ultimate Question translated in the myth, was for him a journey through anguish. Having chosen for myself the angel of Gethsemane, I am wary of the trap of purity. I believe that it was that which trapped the poet, son of Léonard, and mathematician even in his philosophy. He could not conceive suffering and death as basic elements of Life in its fullness, neither could he conceive the dialogue of coexistent opposites in God himself. From this comes his God whose light—a Mediterranean light—is icy, who might be worried of being such as he is, who sees himself weeping in man, does not cry, and knowing all, does not understand. True or false purity, pure purity or impure purity. . . .

Chapter Three

ACCEPTING THE GOSPEL

To accept the Gospel is no easy matter. The humility of God which is evident in it, is recognized as the "pearl" worthy of all sacrifices only after difficult battles in which anything tangible and immediate—as long as the substance seems heavy or beautiful—is at first preferred to this imperceptible eye in which one does not see that all the fires of the world are concentrated. When one wallows in the prestigious waves of sensible matter—I am thinking of *Tristan und Isolde* while I am writing this, I mean the immaterial fluidity of this music in which the impatience of love in the heart of a woman unites itself as if by a miracle with the wind of the night and the birth of a source, disconnected and mingled at the same time—it is hard, it is very hard to give victory to the dry name of Jesus Christ.

No serious tenderness is attached to it, unless it be after a long asceticism, and not always! One has the feeling that he sacrifices reality to a ghost, and that he abandons the feast of life, or even its torment, for an extinct life, a shadow of a shadow. How much more so if one has considered the injustice of the world and has worked to decrease it! Faced with the evidence of scandal and the emergencies of political surgery, it seems that searching the Gospel and obeying its norms takes the bite out of action and gambles with dreams. It is difficult, very difficult for the fighter caught up in the fervor of his fight to close his eyes for a second in order to make sure of the presence of an Image that he fears is already wilted. If someone tells me that he has no ear for music, that the great passions of the flesh and the heart are alien to him or that he knows politics only through the newspapers, I assure him that Therese of Lisieux in her cloister felt, according to one of her biographers, "just as deeply as the unbelievers of our time, this impression of unreality which, at times, seems irresistible when we are faced with the supra-sensible." For her it was a painful trial. For us it is simply the screen of things. Above all, it is the humility of God.

Let neither the ones nor the others be surprised! The humility of God demands that faith be at the peak of our freedom, whatever its ways and stages be. Jesus Christ has no prestige: prestige is always, directly or not, tied to the inessential. In the Gospel, just as in God himself, there is nothing but the essential. The essential is Gratuitousness. Were Jesus Christ more spontaneously desirable to us than amorous passion or science or beauty, he would be the One who can be caught, who can be imprisoned in the net of dreams. Too useful to be God.

The *kenosis* of Christ was total in his death. Which is why this death fully reveals the Glory of God, which is identical to Love as Power of self-annihilation. In Jesus crucified we clearly perceive the pure "for you" negating the "for self" of the living trinitarian Absolute. The cross is the central figure of Revelation: a disfigured man unveils the eternal Being who has no figure. Yet Jesus lived a little more than thirty years. Was he in his not yet disfigured figure a faultless epiphany of the *kenosis* of God? Or should we admit that it was necessary for that human *kenosis* to be limited? Man among men, he had over them an authority that no man ever had; he is not a sinner; he is omniscient.

Starting from an anthropomorphic conception of Glory and Power, inherited from the Old Testament accepted without critique, one could work at discerning what has to be excluded from the kenotic state of Jesus, as being incompatible with his divinity. The problem being thus poorly presented, we will find solutions that, at the conclusion of excessively subtle reasonings, will give of Christ a partially kenotic image. We shall see that a partial *kenosis* of Christ can only reveal a partial *kenosis* of God. As to those who posit from the outset an Absolute without *kenosis*, they can only explain what is kenotic in Christ as an effect of his human will. Then, while continuing to celebrate the humility of Bethlehem and Nazareth, one must cease to talk about the humility of God. And here we come back full circle, for the question remains: what is love? The authority of Jesus? It is affirmed or is perceived in all the pages of the Gospel.

Dodd, alert to shades of meaning and careful not to fall into extrapolations or moralizing excesses, credited it in the end to "an indefinable personal quality."[42] Indefinable? Can we not try—if not to define it with presumption—at least to pinpoint its essential element? I, for one, think that it is humility. For any authority in which one perceives an afterthought or an afterintention is immediately suspicious. The people were not mistaken. There is nothing of that kind in Jesus, even when he strongly affirms, and I dare use the most powerful words: when he "claims" or "pretends"—unique claim, unique pretension—to be able to and to have to say like God: "I am" (Jn 8:58). Were there a chink, no matter how thin, in the humility of Jesus, it would literally be unbearable. I cannot see how this criterion could be challenged. Indeed, it is because the "I am" of Jesus is mysteriously the "I am" of an absolute humility that he unveils the humility of the eternal "I am" of God, and the true nature of his authority.

The impeccability of Jesus? It is not a limitation of *kenosis*.

There would be a contradiction in terms if a sinful Christ, therefore a proud one, were more totally kenotic than a sinless Christ, therefore a humble one. Unless one defines *a priori kenosis* as a participation in the integrality of our sinful condition. But what is precisely the definition of our sinful condition is the original refusal of *kenosis*. The impeccability of Christ is his powerlessness to twist in human acts the Power of self-effacement which is the glory of the Father. Could he sin, he would be a "for self" negating the pure "for you" of God. More kenotic in appearance, he would really betray the *kenosis* of the Absolute.

The omniscience of Jesus? More than one transposes in his humanity the mistaken attribution to God of a knowledge in the mode of having, really distinct from love. I think that it is necessary in order to conquer this phantasm, to accept a certain ignorance on the part of Christ. Most modern theologians agree on this, which encourages me. They say that the criterion of Christ's knowledge is his mission. When the old councils affirm that Christ is not a human person but a divine one, they mean that the humanity of Christ appropriates the existence of the Word in the mode of a singular disappropriation; in other words: that the divine existence is given to it so that it can become communicable. The Word becomes Christ so that Christ can become Church or World. Jesus does not know more than is necessary for him to know for the fulfillment of his mission which is his very being. At least, we can think so without being at odds with Tradition. The *kenosis* of Christ starts in the womb of his Mother, and is consummated on the wood of the cross. Everything in between is *kenosis*.

Jesus was born of an innocent, simple, childlike, crystal-clear woman. These words ring as true as the image that Tradition has drawn of that young mother. Among so many texts written about Mary for nineteen centuries, there is one of Bernanos which expresses so wonderfully what I am trying to say here that I cannot omit quoting it. Let groping words give place to a very pure prose so close to the heart of men that perceive where reality dwells!

> She is our mother, we know that. She is the mother of the human race, the new Eve. But she is also its daughter. The ancient world, the painful world, the world before Grace had nursed her for a long time on its desolate heart—for centuries and centuries—in an obscure and incomprehensible expectation of a *virgo genitrix* . . . For centuries and centuries, the world protected in its old hands laden with crimes, its heavy hands, the wonderful little girl whose name it did not even know. A little girl, this queen of Angels! The Middle Ages had understood it, the Middle Ages understood everything . . . The sanctity of God! The simplicity of God, the frightening simplicity of God which damned the pride of the Angels!
>
> The Virgin had neither triumph nor miracles. Her Son did not permit human glory to touch her, even with the finest tip of its great wild wing. No one has lived, suffered, died as simply and in so deep an ignorance of her own dignity, a dignity that places her yet above the Angels. . . .

If the Angels are not ignorant of their own dignity in the sense Bernanos said that Mary "ignored" hers, is this not why she is above them?

> After all, she was born without sin, what a surprising solitude! A source so pure, so limpid, so limpid and pure that she could not even see in it her reflected image, meant for the sole joy of the Father—o sacred solitude! . . . indeed our poor species is not worth much, but childhood always moves its entrails, the ignorance of the little ones makes it lower its eyes—its eyes that know good and evil, its eyes that have seen so many things.

But this is only ignorance, after all! The gaze of the Virgin is the only truly childish gaze, the only true gaze of a child that ever rose on our shame and misery. Yes, to pray well to her, one must feel this gaze which is not exactly one of indulgence—since indulgence always goes with some bitter experience—but of tender compassion, painful surprise, and another feeling, inconceivable, inexpressible, which makes her younger than sin, younger than the race from which she sprang, and though she be Mother by grace, she is the youngest child of the human race.[43]

Here all is brought together, composed. The eternal childhood of God, and this "painful" surprise which reminds us, in a completely different chord, of the angel of Valéry, and brings childhood close to agony. . . . Childhood and agony together means a fight for the adult. They are the spiritual, or even mystical component of the fight. If mysticism is excluded from ethics, mawkishness creeps in and Jesus is not any more the epiphany of God. Thus his look never ceases to be the look of a child; but of a fighting child, fighting for man. So that man can be. It is a serious look in which many decisions are read. Decisions of a freeman, though this freedom does not go with discernment in the complexity of conjunctures. The agony is within this discernment and these decisions.

It might be good to keep our vocabulary accurate. The *temporal* field is that of *moral* decision. But for one who believes that the living God is actively present in his freedom, the *moral decision* is a *mystical decision*. The *temporal* field is the world in which we are active as freemen: persons, things, events, situations. Persons are always committed to *situations* (family, work, country) and dealing with *events* (familial, professional, political). To think of persons independently from situations and events that condition their history, is to transform them into truly inhuman abstractions. *Situations* and *events* bring into play *values* (justice, honesty, brotherhood, freedom). The world—the *temporal*—is not a sum of *facts* (peace, war, strike) which would only be facts. A strike can be just or unjust. A peace can be obtained at the price of cowardice.

A comfortable station in life can be the fruit of a dishonest subtraction from the national or international income. A labor organization may not care about the rights of the workers. A *moral decision* is one that, brought forth by *facts* (situations or events), aims to bring the triumph of *values* (justice, honesty, truth). It has thus a direct or indirect connection with the *temporal*. No moral decision can be other than a concrete attitude of freedom confronted with the temporal. The *absence of decision* is also, most of the time, a *decision*, just as inertia is a strength. At this level comes the opposition between *morality* and *moralism*. There is *moralism* when conscience, in order to decide, has recourse to a law, given once and for all, a frozen ideal, a sum of principles.

Then there is no need to seek—a key word in Scripture: "Seek and you shall find" (Mt 7:7)—to invent, to analyze the situations in which persons are involved. One is content with finding the pertinent points of the law to apply. Conversely, in a truly *moral* life, conscience understands the law as a creative norm bringing forth personal decisions out of situations that are analyzed as correctly as possible. These decisions constitute a *commitment*. The *values* are then grasped in the decision itself which changes, on a small or large scale, in private as in public life, the course of history. In other words, *moralism* means submission to the law because it is "the law," formal obedience which easily becomes perverted into a respect for usage, of "what is done," and is detrimental to courage, responsibility and "character." *Morality* means *creative fidelity* through the mediation of the law, assuming the law in decisions which express the deepest I.

Many people, who rightly detest moralism because they

perceive its infantilism though they cannot always analyze its causes, tend to belittle, in the name of *spirituality* (or *mysticism*) the truly moral values. This is an aberration. For, if all men are led to moralism by a breach between the temporal and the moral orders, a breach between morality and mysticism in a Christian leads to a scattering of both morality and mysticism. The Gospel is not free of this complexity. How could one remain above the complexity and not integrate it and still see the Gospel as a norm for all men, whatever be their form of combat? The life of Jesus is a network of decisions brought forth by circumstances and inspired by the Spirit. In him obedience and freedom coincide. Humility is at the root. It would be vain to see in his actions the slightest after-intention of a "for self," which is why his discernment is infallible.

Jesus decides to receive baptism at the hands of John. A decision of humility. But at what level? It would twist the impact of this gesture and make it mawkish if it were only the effect of condescension: the sinless man mingling with the crowd of sinners in the waters of the river, even though this is not his place. His place is above; he comes down because he wants to do so. If such were the humility of Jesus, such would be the humility of God. And such would be the incarnation: a "virtuous" decision of the Most-High. If we do not hold back our imagination to prevent it from slipping to such representations, suspicion—even at the ethical level—enters in. For humility, understood in such a way, is questionable. Humility is pure only if it is not sought after and wanted for itself.

The humility of God is his mode of being; and so it is with Jesus. And God *is* in the mode of *being-with*. Between "being-with" and "bending toward" there is a chasm. Jesus does not bend toward the sinners: he is with them. He does not leave his own place, he points out to it. Because he is sinless, his solidarity with sinful mankind has no shadow of pride; it is thus total and genuine. There is no sham. No sham either in the temptation to which he is subjected. Jesus experiences the fact that "to bend toward" would apparently be more efficient than "to be with." But one does not bend toward freedoms without already starting to grasp them, thus to destroy them. The mediocre man lets himself be wounded in his freedom by trampling on his dignity. The suggestions of Satan in the desert of Judea are, in fact, our own suggestions.

The God who respects us is not the one we would want him to be, at least when bad dreams impel us to prefer happiness to freedom and to accept a servile tranquility. There are so many forms of gilded slavery! An abundance of bread, or "economy first"; a celestial afterlife guaranteed by the manifestation of its existence and power, thus imposing itself in such a way that doubting would be stupid; a religion so tightly linked with traditions and customs that it is best to belong to it. These are the main aspects of a "usefulness" of God. Jesus, precisely because he "is with" the sinners, lives from the inside, without committing their sin. This intimate contradiction between experience and mission is called temptation by the Gospel. This means that at any moment, Jesus sees—because men give him to see—what would be captive freedom and what should be respected—therefore saved—freedom. He is the Savior. Savior of what? Of man? Of what in man? Of that which makes man what he is: freedom. He thus refuses triumphs so that Gratuitousness can be, remain and reign. Such is the humble and sorrowful Servant of created freedom, therefore of the God who creates it, who had been announced by the second Isaiah. Humility respects, usefulness does not.

The teaching of Jesus, especially in the Sermon on the Mount which sums it up, has no other goal than to bring us back, as freedom, our lost natural childhood. "Unless you change and become like little children you will never enter the kingdom of heaven" (Mt 18:3). From childlike nature to childlike freedom, the passage is in the shape of death and resurrection. In order to become what we are, children of God, the eternal childhood of the Father—which we call Grace—must tear us away from the determinisms of aging. We cling to them: it is his agony and ours. Childhood is only at the peak of freedom if we are the child of someone: it is not a state in itself, but the quality of a relation. It is ours only if the One whose child we are is more Child than us. If the "Eternal childhood of God" were spoiled by a crease, I mean by this if God were not an infinity of humility, we could not be his children, with all that this implies of confidence, abandonment, joy and respect. The suspicion that would arise in us would not be a sin like that of Adam for it would be God himself, a God who would not be God, that would arouse it.

Thus Jesus cannot invite us to enter childhood unless he reveals a God who is childhood without flaw. The father of the prodigal son is more purely childlike in his greeting than the son is in his return. Not a single iota of rancor. The still imperfect humility of the son will be able to go forth to meet the unlimited humility of the father. "You must therefore be perfect," Jesus says, "as your heavenly Father is perfect" (Mt 5:48). Man cannot attain the perfection of God except by never ceasing to strive for it. But the demand is such that it can only be understood as a call to freedom! There is a correlation between the radical demand and the total freedom of the response. Thus one can neither lower its price nor settle it. The Gospel does not give moral orders: it is normative. The aim of the disciple transcends the ethical order, but it has to be achieved in ethical decisions which pertain to his freedom. This is what Jesus said all along in his days on earth, until it became perfectly clear that it is not possible to be only decent with a Crucified One.

Miracle ceases being repulsive to me when I grasp its tie of solidarity with the non-miracle. In the Gospel the refusal of miracle is at the forefront; the acceptance of miracle is at the background, but they are superimposed one on the other. Jesus who heals the sick is the very same Jesus who, at the threshold of his ministry, refused to change stones into bread and who, tomorrow on the cross, will recognize the presence of the Father only in the mode of silence and absence. Between the first and the final scene, all the life of Jesus is marked with the seal of the non-intervention of God. In this, his death is constantly prophesied. It is thus that his thaumaturgical activity paradoxically unfolds. It has the same style as his word. And the latter is at the point of silence. It breaks silence to reveal the kenotic depth of God. It was born of silence—thirty years of obscurity, and during public life, whole nights of solitude and prayer—and returns to silence when, on Calvary, Father and Son are both silent.

But this silence is neither remoteness nor opacity. The word qualifies it precisely as the very essence of Reality in its proximity. The word says that silence is not nothingness but fullness. Hence, the miracle. In order for the non-miracle to reveal the ultimate secret of love, miracle must be seen through the seeming absence of Glory by pointing to what glory truly is: concern for man, care for him, "sweet pity" for him, power to cure, forgiveness. In a painting of Vermeer, the essential is what one guesses or senses through what is shown: the perceptible unsaid beyond the said. The immobile gesture of a reading woman, the sun caressing a city about to awake, the yellow and blue turban on a young head: one can talk about "miracles of art," such is the overwhelming proof that deep secrets are shivering here in an invisible "inside" to which one gains access through the extreme restraint of the "outside." The same holds true for Jesus touching the eyes of a blind man or raising up a paralytic one: we can hear God's heart beating. Jesus does not invite us to see prodigious things. Not a hint of stage management. Nothing prepared beforehand. Jesus does not blow his trumpet. And he strictly enjoins the cured people not to blow it either (Mk 1:43-44). Even if Mark has described this with some systematic rigidity, the "messianic secret" draws around the miracles a ring of *kenosis*.

Before unveiling in the non-miracle of death its most intimate mystery, the Power of God walks in the streets and byways, on squares and temple areas, concerned with the life of men in its simplest and most concrete forms. It suffers in their sufferings and rejoices in imparting to them immediate strength and elementary joy. A miracle testifies to a sensitive and throbbing God who seizes us at our lowest point to raise us to the highest one. The supreme demand of live will be one of transformation and exaltation, for if God became man it was for man to become God. But God made man does not despise the humble beginnings of his desiring creature. He meets it in those areas where its flesh is at its most carnal and where its appetites are spontaneously revealed. He removes what burdens the creature: leprosy, paralysis, blindness, hunger. If I read the Gospel by taking in the same look miracle and non-miracle, I grasp the humility of God which is present and active at all levels of his desire and ours.

It is true that the episode of the Transfiguration shows that the glory of God is present and hidden in the humility of the man Jesus. But it reveals also, and especially so, that the humility of the man Jesus is the heart of the glory of God. The tearing of the veil shows not only that God has temporarily taken in Jesus the shape of a servant, but also, and above all, that the shape of a servant, appearing in Jesus, is the eternal shape of God. In that scene, everything is centered on the coming Passion. First the context in the Synoptic Gospels, before and after. A few days earlier, Jesus had announced for the first time that he would be rejected, would have to suffer and die. Yet he had declared himself to be the Son of Man of whom Daniel spoke (Dn 7:13-14): "coming on the clouds of heaven" and who would receive for centuries "sovereignty, glory and kingship." He reproached Peter who had been scandalized by such an intolerable identification of the glorious Son of Man and the Suffering Servant of Isaiah. He added that no one could be his disciple unless he renounced himself and took up his cross (Mk 8:31-38).

Going down the mountain, Jesus—according to Matthew —repeats the announcement of his sufferings. Prophesied before and after, the Passion is also evoked during the Transfiguration. It is Luke who stresses this: Moses and Elijah talking about the passing Jesus was to accomplish in Jerusalem (Lk 9:30-31). All the details of the narration bring to mind the theophanies of the Old Testament: the mountain is high, as were Sinai and Horeb; Moses is present—the man of Sinai— and Elijah—the man of Horeb; the clothes of Jesus are dazzling white; his face shines like the sun; a voice is heard from within the luminous cloud which is that of Exodus. Everything says: this is God. Thus God is the one who is going to suffer and die so that the very being of his glory will be revealed in its fullness. This page of the Gospel must be understood in all its dimensions. I believe it to be true that Jesus wanted to lessen the scandal of a painful and humiliated Messiah whom people had expected to be triumphant. It is also true that his transfiguration was an anticipation of his resurrection. What is essential is that the witnesses of the Glory on the mountain will be tomorrow the witnesses of the holy weakness of Christ in the Garden, and that between this weakness and that glory there is no opposition but indestructible unity. The pedagogical style of the theophanies bows before the absolute absence of style which, at Gethsemane, announces clearly who God is. "This is my body offered, this is my blood poured out." The extreme simplicity of these words and the gesture which accompanies them, is the image of God's incomprehensible simplicity. What he had first manifested in announcing the Good News, by uniting himself to the multiple aspects of human complexity,

Jesus brings into the Last Supper, without excluding anything, in a rite bordering on insignificance. For it is only a form of insignificance that can signify the abysmal depth of Glory's humility. All that would pertain to explanation and feelings, far from revealing God, would hide him. Jesus, at the most ardently desired hour of his life, rigorously abstains from such things: "My body . . . given up for you . . . blood of the covenant poured out for all . . . take . . . eat . . . drink": nothing else, no matter what the differences are between the four narrations. There is only the essential.

When the essential clothes itself in insignificance, the risk is that it will remain unperceived. Then one slips into banality. But there is another risk if one resorts to teachings in which the eminently significant value of the form of insignificance could vanish. It is true that the Eucharist must be a feast for those who participate in it: and man can have a feast only when his environment contains sensible elements in a prominent way. But what makes human feasts possible beyond delusions and precariousness, is the fact that Jesus offered his body and poured out his blood. The Eucharistic feast, because it is the condition of any feast, is itself of a completely different order, and it is unique in its own order. In the same way that a "useful" God will never cease to be suspected by the very people who have "used" him, a liturgy too indiscreetly removed from the restrained, modest and austere, filled with a false splendor alien to Jesus' intentions, would sooner or later become suspicious to the very people for whom it would have been prepared artificially. The healthily educated man, Fenelon said, "has the same taste as God." Such words are not aristocratic: they show a respect for the people.

The resurrection of Jesus is not a clearly prodigious event. If it were so, where would be the freedom of faith? Could we still believe in the humility of a God who would constrain our reason? Or would we have to declare as uneducated, ignorant or in bad faith those who claim to escape from this constraint? In fact, the post-Paschal Gospel only proposes modest signs inviting to faith. No one has seen Jesus leaving the tomb. He does not show himself in the process of resurrection. He simply teaches his disciples how to recognize him as resurrected. Here we are at the extreme opposite of mythologies. There is nothing that could evoke a dead god avenging himself, dazzling those who killed him in a splendid victory. If we disregard the texts and slip into this kind of representation, we make God in our image, transposing to him our aggressiveness and our unhealthy dream of a history from which one could escape through supra-terrestial wonders.

The resurrected Jesus entrusts the apostles with the mission of testifying to his freedom. He lived as a free man. He died because he remained free. Once resurrected, it is clear to the eyes of faith that the very freedom of God was the source of his human freedom and that he never put any obstacle to its springing forth from the depths of his being. No risk therefore that he will trap our freedom after having gone to the extremes of love in order to save it! Thus he does not change our life in its multiform conditioning, since a created liberty can only create itself by going through the ways of night, determinism and violence. But he promises the Spirit and gives him, so that the Energy of love that made him free can also make us free like him so that we become his brothers in freedom.

The resurrected Jesus does not show the glow of his Glory. How could he, since the most glowing point of divine Incandescence is the power of love which, far from showing itself, is self-effacing? When, after a radical transformation, we will be ourselves in the heart of Fire, *the identity—understood at last—of humility and of the splendid flashing light will be our adoring joy*. This is why Jesus appears to his disciples under the laws of the human condition, in the reality of a Glory which to them has the shape of a shadow. If God were not humble, his forgiveness would be suspicious and we would have the right to wonder whether it would not be greater to refuse it than to accept it. Suspicion cannot overshadow the giving of pardon without equally overshadowing its acceptance. Here and there humility is the absolute condition of authenticity. If we doubt whether God is humble when he forgives, we will be led to doubt whether we are humble when we praise him. Gratitude is valid only as an homage to the gratuitousness of the gift. Otherwise no relationship of truth could be possible between man and God. The same would hold true between men because if their common sonship is broken, their brotherhood is also broken at the root: men cannot live together if they do not forgive one another for being only what they are.

God needs more power to forgive than to create. More precisely, his power of forgiveness is interior to his creative power, as a super-power of re-creation. By creating freedoms God commits himself in an increase of love—excess is his very being—to restore to them, if they let it wither, the power he gives them to create themselves. This commitment is inscribed in the Trinitarian "sacrifice": since the beginning of the world the Lamb is slain, the Word is eternally impressed on creation in the shape of a cross. Pardoning is truly in God as a perfection of gift. If God the creator is not a Star giving himself satellites, God the re-creator is even less so. By restoring freedoms to themselves, he shows a humbler love than when he brings them forth. No looking down, no trace of this high-handedness, which in our human ways of forgiving is a hidden form of calculation or contempt. God is alien to this type of friendship that André Gide calls "devaluating": that is, loaded with condescension and protection, which makes one feel even in the depth of intimacy that the beloved is not equal to the lover.

Here one should tell, in order to show what God's forgiveness is not, all the degrading forms of human pardon, irritating, cajoling, or debasing depending on the case, such as experience shows them: the pleasure of feeling oneself superior to the offender by abstaining from revenge; subtle selfishness; political calculation; idealistic evasion and all the shades of resentment. The forgiveness of God is an act: the death of Jesus Christ. This act tells what his being is. The awareness of my unworthiness is such that forgiveness is more necessary to me than bread. Alone with myself, I am disgusted by being what I am. Talking with a God who is humbler than I am, every minute of my life is a re-birth to creative Gratuitousness: the human task is without limit. This is what I am trying to share, as best as I can and in a brotherly way, with my contemporaries.

Part II

THE SUFFERING OF GOD

The Father Himself
is not Impassible

Origen

Chapter Four

SPONTANEITY

At the threshold of a small book which I foresee as over-loaded with question marks—it is possible for God to suffer? Can one conceive him as not suffering?—I want to print as an affirmation without reservation the word JOY: eternal joy of God, joy hoped for by men. This word is essential to my faith. Though there are days when nothing seems to be able to escape a semblance of derision, nothing yet can prevent at the very moment—an effort to smile becomes twisted into a pucker—the survival of hope, stronger than sadness. Every morning that God makes, be the sky bright or dark, my heart heavy or light, I respond to the liturgical Invitatory: "Come, let us sing joyfully." Every evening, whether the thought of death brought forth by the night be sweet or cruel to me, I obey the Church that impels us to whisper—always in the plural form—at the end of her prayer to Mary, the words which call to each other: joy—*laetamur*—and freedom—*liberemur*.

Thus our days follow each other closely linked to the image of life in the width of its span: the priest who baptized me asked God "that I serve him joyfully in his Church"; the priest who will attend my last agony will advise me that with "a face of rejoicing," Christ is near. Between the morning and the evening of the day, between the morning and the evening of life, verses from the psalms bring to me, as a hum constantly accompanying work and play, the echo of the immemorial

Jewish rejoicing: "In joy we walk towards You.... Serve God in joy ... Go to Him with songs of joy." Many a time, during the heavy hours when all is lead inside and outside, when the crudeness of things and the exhaustion of the mind preclude all music, I have asked Saint Paul to whisper into my ear the incredible sentence he had written to the Romans (8:18): "I think that what we suffer in this life can never be compared to the glory, as yet unrevealed, which is waiting for us." And I have also prayed Jesus to confirm to my tense contemporaries the promise made to the apostles: "Your hearts will be full of joy, and that joy no one shall take from you" (Jn 16:22).

Please God, let no discourse—even in the questioning mode—lead men to doubt this Ocean of beatitude whose supreme Existence is the supreme reason for life and hope! A friend worried when she heard me talk about a possible eternal suffering of God, and I must answer her in reassuring words: "I am divorced," she said, "I have suffered and I suffer much, I have known degradation, exile, failure. I have faced death several times, mine and that of very dear people. I have felt in myself hatred, revolt and despair. Yet, as I go from pain to pain, I am more confident that Joy exists and that we must dance for joy in the joy of God. You want to talk about his suffering? Would his joy still be far then?" On the contrary, it is very close, at least if I manage to show that the highest beatitude—that of God, that which we are hoping for—far from excluding suffering, mysteriously implies it. Do not worry, my friend, I will not contradict Kierkegaard who noted in his *Journal* that: "any man who really wants to be in relationship with God and be so often, has only one thing to do: always be joyful." And it is certainly in the depths of my soul and not only on the stage and in orchestral music that I hear the voices greeting the dying Joan of Arc: "There is joy which is the strongest." Yet, one must dare to use paradox.

When it comes to God, we may suspect anything that does

not have a paradoxical aspect. Father de Lubac has entitled *Paradoxes* one of his best books—stripped of all erudition—saturated with lived and reflected spiritual experience. He writes: "The very word 'paradox' is paradoxical. Let it keep its paradox. . . . Let us also remember that the Gospel is full of paradoxes, that man himself is a living paradox, and that—according to the Fathers of the Church—the Incarnation is the supreme Paradox, *Paradoxos paradoxon.*"[44] And to prevent any possible equivocation, he stresses: "There are paradoxes of expression: one exaggerates in order to 'make the most of.' And there are real paradoxes. The latter presuppose an antinomy; a truth that shocks us is balanced by another truth. It does not limit it, but only locates it. We will not say: 'That's all it was.' Paradoxical truth is not limited. Which is why, most of the time, neither Jesus nor Saint Paul balances the paradox. They fear mad interpretation less than another understanding that would degrade it and deprive it of its 'heroism.'"[45]

The paradox of a humble God seemed violent to more than one reader. And here is the paradox of a suffering God, even more violent. Is it true that suffering, like humility, is at the heart of Glory? To come near such a mystery, one must first become—as Bachelard puts it: "as serious as a dreaming child." Then one should before crossing the threshold of the discourse, convince oneself as did Kierkegaard—without excess though—that paradox is "a category of understanding." One should, above all, at the very thought that God might suffer, be seized by a suffering which, however feeble it be, would be a sharing in his. For if God suffers, it cannot be with a vague emotion, marginal as it were, and barely touching him without taking hold of him.

There is nothing accidental in God. If God suffers, his suffering is as big as his being and his joy, dimension without dimension, limitless, infinite. At the heart of Essence and according to the immeasurable amplitude of his radiance. I will ask Bachelard how one can manage to be "as serious as a dreaming child": he knows how to say it wonderfully. I will listen to the teaching of the philosophers and theologians: with their reasoning reason does not turn against the mind; they warn us—without however slipping into fideism—that a science of God ends up necessarily in nescience. But there is this which I cannot positively want or even desire: the experience of a participation in the suffering of God. It can only be a theopathy. In the double meaning of the word: not only to "suffer God," as do all the mystics—*ta theia pathein*—but to suffer his suffering—*ta pathe tou Theou pathein*. Already beyond this possible deepening of the abyss, I have learned that an "intention of mysticism," as Jacques Paliard puts it, is "destructive of mysticism: indeed it substitutes for it an aestheticism of spirituality."[46]

This is a place where delusions are rife. I must therefore, when talking about a God who might suffer, resign myself to the suffering of not suffering, remaining watchful so as not to allow myself to ever be delighted by what would be an increase of knowledge—the act of writing is never pure—as if the stammering quest for the Inexpressible could in itself fill the gap between me and me, the superficial me manipulating concepts and the deep me where God dwells! Let your book—a young woman tells me—be the child of the desert! Well said. But still, how bitter it is to accept this compulsory dryness when I think that Dostoyevsky was sick from emotion when he looked at Holbein's painting in the Museum of Basel which represents the dead body of Christ being taken off the cross! At that moment, the great novelist escaped from what he called "the normal terrestrial order," meaning the easy balance of existence in its banality, devoid of tragedy, depth and mystery. If at least, I were hit straight in the face—and my reader along with me—by the gravity on the face of God! It must be possible. But Hegel was right when he dreaded mediocre art which "gives to platitude the appearance of a profound discourse."

The image of an impassible God looking down, with olympic serenity, on the evil and the misery of the world remains and pursues its secret existence in the depths of mankind's unconscious. "Impassible" means "insensitive," therefore "indifferent" if we ignore or refuse the subtle game of the *distinguo*, which after all, even when it lets us bring some nuances to the idea, leaves the image and its dynamic power intact. How can one believe that God is love if one must think that our suffering does not reach him in his eternal being? When I weep or degrade myself, is he "absolute marble"? Love is vulnerable but a perfect nature is not. God is perfect, unless he is not really God. This is why, for many people, the image of a Being that nothing can hurt coexists—though not without a secret revolt—with the historical reality of a brotherly Christ who suffered and died on the cross. The suffering of Christ, far from softening the scandal of the impassibility of the Father and the Spirit, would rather seem to increase it. For it would not only be the suffering of the creatures that would be unable to move the Eternal but also the suffering of the one the Father sent, the Son made man, suffering in such agony that his sweat turned to blood while the Absolute would not have even shivered in his eternally blissful being!

Jesus suffered only once; human suffering is always with us. It is now that I suffer, it was in the past that he carried his cross. Now he is glorious. Sitting at the bedside of a man dying of cancer, his face ravaged by the disease and yet never stopping to breathe, the most Christian of wives can utter this complaint that one would be very foolish to call blasphemous: "For Christ, it lasted only a few hours; for you, months!" What a tragic derision, when one hears this, to try and argue about the relationship between time and eternity! Nothing can prevent me, when I am bent under a burden, from imagining the happiness of God and his Christ as being without flaw. How powerful is the unconscious! How tenacious the phantasms it brings forth! Jacques Maritain, a few years before his death, indicated that "a metaphysical psychoanalysis of the modern world would put the finger on the evil that ravages its unconscious. If only people knew... that God 'suffers' with us and far more than we do from all the evil that destroys the earth, many things would undoubtedly change and many souls would be freed."[47]

Of course, his fidelity to Thomism inclined Maritain to stress the "metaphorical" aspect of the word "suffering." We shall see later how he understood it. But the old philosopher was lucid when he evoked this "spiritual despair" which, at times, makes men "rage" against God. "I know," he wrote, "quite a few Christians who prefer not to think about it and who, through a kind of dichotomy due to a total ignorance of theology and to the absurdities of a sickly 'cryptogamic' rationalization have on the one hand a vague notion (at least these words were told to them) that God is Love, and on the other hand think about Him, not as they would about a Father ... but as an Emperor of this world, a Potentate-Dramatist who would—thanks to a self-given permission to fail *preceding* our weaknesses and to abandon his creature to itself from the outset—be the first author of all the sins of the world and of all its miseries, and who would enjoy the spectacle staged by himself of a human history abominably full of evil. It is this absurd and intolerable image of the Potentate-Dramatist insensitive in his heaven to the suffering of the characters playing in his theater, which is lurking at the bottom of the rebellion against God of the great mass of the non-Christians."

All that I love in this world—a tree, a rose, a bird, the birth of a smile, the life of the spirit—I cannot doubt that God loves it even more. All that is impossible for me to love—the harm I inflict on my brothers and that which they inflict on me, injustice, misery, thirst, hunger; disease which attacks, ravages, breaks and destroys—will I say that God contemplates it serenely because the perfection of his immutable nature forbids him to tremble? Christ, it is true, trembled unto death. But the Father? And the Spirit? And I would rather not say anything here of the tortured child, the humiliated innocent. Naively, without having the slightest suspicion about the whims of my imagination, I like to compare the Infinite Being to an Aeolian harp that the faintest breath of human joy or suffering moves and causes to vibrate. I would not want, when going on to reflection, to sacrifice this image. I am haunted by the word *adventure*, and I am upset at the idea that I might also be asked to give it up.

Creative work is an adventure. God ventured. He took a risk. He opened up for men a road to freedom strewn with dangers. And if it is now that God creates, it is now that he ventures, that he accepts the possibility—the reality—of tears and blood. Not only our tears and our blood! Not only the tears and the blood of Christ! Would the Creator stand aside? Can there be, can there not be, at the heart of the pure Spirit, something unnameable which can analogically be compared to our tears and our blood?

When a question is essential, mysterious and arduous, it is simply honest to first confess that we are embarrassed. To decide too quickly would be a cheap way to create a delusion of clarity. It would be falling into the temptation of facility, of which the great artists, poets and philosophers know to beware. "Easy things are fatal," says René Char. One must be all the more severe with one's mind and pen because we are living in days of overkill and exclusivism. The *Magisterium*, aware of having abused in the past the argument of authority, is reasonably hesitant to use it now in order to calm the excesses and cut short the many half-baked novelties.

In the field of literary critique, people have spoken of "clean-ups which are dirtying." It also holds true in theology:

excess of negativism, systematic refusal of anthropomorphism, replacement of one anthropomorphism by another which people are incapable of seeing as leading to the worst. Of these "dirtying" games, Claude Bruaire gives a typical example: "Religion," he says, "would have given way to a beguiling anthropomorphism by finding a substitute for "the Father" as a name for the Absolute. Obsessed from birth by its progenitor, in a complex of desire and hatred, consciousness would fantastically project on the shadow of God the name of the Father that haunts it. To the extent that the believers are invited to purify their faith by exorcising the paternity of the divine! Yet, it is easy to understand why such a purification can only lead to atheism. Far from fitting human procreation, paternity is a *univocal concept* which revokes our paternities. Because what it means exactly is *the Father*, namely, the *father without father*. And this, no man can ever be, quite simply because he is first a son, because he is not absolute and creative Origin, beginning without beginning. Far from it being anthropomorphic to call God our Father, it is by manifest theomorphism that any progenitor is usurping this divine Name."[48]

An impassible God? A God who suffers? Which is the most dangerous of the two anthropomorphisms? Already, here and there, the topic is studied without the necessary care, without a sufficient concern for a balance to keep. If we have to prefer an approximation, let it be the one that is the worthiest of God! Such will not be decided without our having to go down to this deepest point of man where heart and mind are closely knit in faith.

Quite often, the thought of an eternally suffering God has helped me not to sin against gratuitousness. I firmly believe that many will know God and will be forever united with him, even though they had not even suspected in their days on this earth the existence of an infinitely loving being. The very name of Jesus Christ is unknown to multitudes. It happens that Christians accept this without too much concern. When the theology of "the salvation of the unbelievers" was abrupt and summary, when one was not afraid to sentence to damnation or limbo all the unbaptized, the Church had a devouring missionary zeal. It was, for the souls, a matter of life or death. Less narrow, and more enlightened, we have perhaps become more tepid. If the "implicit" is enough, the passage to "explicit" seems less urgent.

And it remains true that man is not gifted in discerning what the faith of his brothers means in God's eyes, what is, according to the Gospel, its salvific reality: therefore we cannot judge. But I cannot refuse to believe, without failing myself in my own faith, that God wants from all eternity for all mankind to attain the explicit knowledge of the one he sent, Jesus Christ. "Make disciples of all the nations" (Mt 28:19). I am thus entitled to think that any lazy slowness, any negligence, any shortcoming of energy to make the Son known and loved, hurts the Father and saddens the Spirit. This should be enough to gratuitously feed a flame in me. It should also introduce a note of quasi-carnal affliction in my sympathy for the intelligence manifested by the modern world in its research and in its very unbelief. God accompanies the scientist, the philosopher and the politician on their way. He is with them, but they are not always with him, and his respectful love prevents him from intervening when their steps stray; when bad faith shows through good faith; when timidity, prejudices or dreams become stronger than wisdom and courage; when evolution is regression. To participate with a full heart in the motion of the world, from the viewpoint of God's suffering—and also of his joy—what light for discerning the truth! The Marquis de Sade, who had dug into the archives of Cythera, reaped the fruit of his investigation by stating simply: "In this world, one esteems only that which is gain or pleasure."

Whether in or out of Cythera, when it comes to ideology or practicality, it is true that the useful is king. It is a constant trait of our Western civilization that man is, in all fields, used for ends that are lower than himself. In order to estimate the price of the gratuitousness essential to love, philosophers and theologians would have to work together with poets.

"Birds that we stone at the pure moment of your vehemence, where are you falling?" If I were a professor of theology, I would like to propose this admirable verse of René Char to the students as the theme of a paper or dissertation. And I would rejoice if one of them, uniting the spirit of childhood and the intelligence of the phrase "food for thought," were to suggest that God looks for these birds, finds them, and sadly caresses them. Francis of Assisi, Therese of Lisieux, called forth at the conclusion of a rigorous discourse: what a beautiful lesson for the wise ones, who in the name of wisdom, believe that they have to repudiate madness! An invulnerable Father would be a Father without tenderness. It is the *tenerezza* of God that lets me stand before him as a child and talk about him as children do. The time will come for critique and argumentation. Simplicity, unconcerned by anthropomorphism, comes first and will be reconquered later.

Thus I am happy, at this point in my book, to echo the song of Julien Clerc: "Don't cry like this, you make the good God cry." In our iron century, these naive words remind us that some fire has survived the cold of the ashes. The popular soul hides this fire. "Don't make the good God sad": what sentence could you coin that would better express what could truly be the apex of gratuitousness? "Do this, my little one, to please the good God": if something human can please him, certain things can also displease him. How can we doubt that it is possible to displease Someone we love and who loves us? And what would be a displeasure without sadness? "I thought a great deal about you when you lost your wife": this is either a banal utterance of politeness or it means, if I am talking to a friend, that I have suffered with him when I thought about him. If God is in me more me than me, if it is from the inside and not from the height of an observatory that he sees my misery and my sin, is there not in his heart a rebound when I miss a step at the edge of the abyss? In truth, he does not see me, he touches me. He did not even smile when I stumbled seriously. Neither did he assume a severe expression, like a school teacher who owes it to himself to frown while remaining indifferent.

I attach here the letter of a mother moved by the idea of God's vulnerability: "When my children were small, when I thought for them, everything was easy: my freedom was the only one on the line. But when the time came for me to realize that my role was to accustom them to progressive choices, I felt—as soon as I consented to this—that worry had settled with me. By letting my children make decisions, therefore take risks, I was myself by the same token taking the risk of seeing the emergence of freedoms other than my own. If, too often, I continued to choose in the place of my children, it was—I must confess—in order to spare them the suffering of an option they might have to regret later; but it was at least, if not at most, in order not to risk facing the trial of a disagreement between their choice and the one I would have wanted them to make. Lack of love on my part thus: because acting in such a way, I basically wanted to spare myself a possible suffering, the one I have felt each time my children took another way than the one I considered to be the best for them. Thus I can perceive that God 'the Father' can suffer. We are his children. He wants us free to build ourselves by ourselves, and the Infinity of his love prevents any constraint on his part. Perfect love, devoid of any trace of calculation, implying the acceptance from the outset of a suffering inherent to this total freedom he wants us to have."

To believe in a suffering God is to make the mystery more

mysterious, though in a more luminous way. It is to chase away a false clarity to replace it with glowing darkness. It is perhaps also to strengthen man when the blackest of his demons attack him, against the temptation of being jealous of God. The project of the modern world, I know, is antitragic. Is it opportune to dramatize God himself? Does not the idea of a suffering God aggravate the scandal by amplifying it to infinity? Does it not lead to this "generalized injustice" of which Camus said that at the times of triumphant faith was "as satisfying to man as total justice," and made possible a "strange happiness"?[49] Unless it describes very precisely the locus of the most radical choice: compact absurdity or abysmal gratuitousness? In any event, talking here about timeliness is not serious.

Chapter Five

THE BIBLE

First, we must question Scripture. A Jewish reading of the Bible does not lead to a recognition of Jesus as Messiah, Son of God, center of history. A Christian reading leads to recognizing him as such. However, on either side the image of a pathetic God asserts itself. For André Neher,[50] the first page of Genesis offers the picture of a perfect, accomplished creation, being fulfilled and blossoming. But soon there are loopholes, gaps, an "inversion of supplements and surpluses." Some creatures resist God; there are adventures, revolts, dramas. Thus it seems that the creative work "was in no way meditated or achieved through a pre-established plan, but to the contrary, that it came forth out of a radical lack of preparation, keeping all along its realization the now disappointing and now stimulating traits of an improvization." No label of guarantee! Radical insecurity from the outset! Ulterior history gives the measure of the consequences: "It is a sum of failures and remorses, a dramatic game full of improvizations of which the central and unhappy hero is God." The Creator seeks his creatures. "Where are you?", he says to Adam hiding behind the trees. From one end to the other of the Old Testament, this call resounds: "It is the weak echo," says Abraham Heschel,[51] "of a weak voice, never expressed in words, never translated into categories of understanding, inexpressible and mysterious, as inexpressible and mysterious as the glory filling the whole world. Muted, muffled, it is wrapped in silence, but it is as if all things were the frozen echo of the question: *Where are you?*" If the divine work is improvised, it is under the sign of uncertainty. The game is open. There is an irreducible perhaps. Risk of failure is permanent. No Omega point which would bring together in a final fullness the infinite fragments of the previous failures and would reunite them in a finally comprehensible figure, as would a magnet drawing filings into a magnetic field. God can lose his creatures; there is a painful gap between the divine intention and its failure. Such are, for André Neher, the conditions of a genuine hope, the hope sung by Jeremiah, "the hope of a Good Friday which knows that it will never hear the bells of Easter Sunday." "In the Jewish language of the XIIIth century, it is the hope of martyrdom without miracle. . . . Transposed in the Jewish history of the XXth century, it is *the hope of Auschwitz.*"

In the stream of biblical images, Neher grasps those that depict a God dramatically uncertain about the success of his work. I do not know by which reflective way he criticizes its anthropomorphism, neither how he conceives "this inexhaustible cistern of the Being" of which he says that human hope "fortifies itself," "by finding in it a new breath," even in the possibility of "a final wreck" of history. In any case, I can see that he pleads against Christianity and for gratuitousness. For him, the bells of Easter—Christology—close history into its center in such a way that spaces and times are "lit up from beginning to end, without any remains of shadow, if not mystery." Thus the promise is fulfilled, and the reward won. But "fulfillment is the suicide of promise," and reward the negation of disinterest. One must "give up totally any utopia of reward or approval." If the bells of Easter were a denial of gratuitousness, our duty would be indeed to stop our ears in order not to hear. Christians listen to them because they sing of the absolute disinterest of joy. We call Grace the offer of an increased gratuitousness, access to God's own way of loving. Our hope is for a love finally stripped of self-interest. If we talk of beatitude as a reward, it is only when we mean that the idea of reward has no room in the hearts of the saints. This concerns our differences. Here I only want to stress the points on which we meet. A Judeo-Christian dialogue starting from these perspectives of extreme height can, I believe, keep in the forefront the image of a pathetic God, accepted on either side. The Jewish and Christian readings of the Bible agree, for instance, on the following, which is fundamental.

"The *Ruah* of God . . . is pathetic. It is a truth that no idealism, no spirituality can soften, let alone erase. The fact that only one word, the same one, *ruah* defines in the Bible the highest spiritual dimension, the most detailed one, and also psychic life in its ultimate contradictions, was only possible within the context of a pathetic conception of the Spirit. The Greeks were not able to reach this concept. Their philosophers deemed motions, and consequently emotions, incompatible with divinity . . . The Hebrews on the contrary, saw in history and its motions, a manifestation of their God; the emotions of God were the springs of this history of which men were the unavoidable actors. The emotion of God was imprinted in the very condition of man. The Biblical description of God is, to be sure, anthropopathic. This means that God appeared to Biblical man in the polarity of his *pathos*, in his love and in his anger, in his severity and in his forgiveness. The *ruah* of God judges itself: it repents. This repentance of God would be enough to show that the Biblical God is not tied to an abstract and general principle. It is not the God of universal principles, but the God of Unicity, of the historical moment. The *ruah* is not spiritual fixity, but vital emotion."[52]

In the vocabulary of the Covenant, the word *hesed* does not have one meaning, but a rainbow of shades of meanings. It expresses the gratuitousness of friendship, at the root of the choice of preference. It also talks about the desire of reciprocity. The behavior that makes exchange possible between people united by a tie: fidelity, generosity, loyalty, confidence. Duty, yet more than duty: one cannot be content with being decent toward a father, brother, friend. Deep sympathy beyond sensible emotion, anticipating the desires of the partner, even when they are not explicitly expressed. God granted his *hesed* to Israel by choosing it as his people: he expects the people to reciprocate by choosing him. One should find here the rich complexity of the Latin word *pietas*, which suggests intimacy, sweetness, respect, intuition of the proper distances that have to be kept. *Rahamim* is close to *hesed* but refers to a more carnal aspect of the tie of reciprocity. *Rahem* means maternal breast, uterus. *Rahamim* therefore evokes the call of the blood with all that it implies in emotion and irrepressible inner turmoil: Joseph meeting his brothers, the true mother discovered in the judgment of Solomon, the father whose heart is moved when the prodigal son comes back, and God himself towards each one of his children. The word does not express exactly suffering, but the warm intimacy of which it is the sign cannot exclude it.

A thousand confessions help me to feel the extreme of Hosea's suffering. When one holds a woman in his arms, heart to heart, and is struggling not to blush with shame as motions of slyness or irony, selfishness or evil are felt through the carnal shell of the beloved, one touches an infernal depth of distress. *I love you and you are not worthy to be loved.* In order to live, one should be able to forget. To erase, at least to accept distraction and sing the lullabies of delusion. *"Odi tua, amote,"* says Saint Augustine: "I hate your works, I love you." These words have an abysmal depth. It is the God of Hosea who voices them with tears. In the very name of God, Jeremiah laments: "If you do not listen to this warning I will bewail your pride in secret, tears will flood my eyes, for Yahweh's flock is led into captivity" (Jr 13:17).

This God in tears is holy. The simplicity of his innocence is as terrible as fire. What is an active flame that one ought to console? The Bible does not attempt a reflected synthesis of the images it offers in abundance. It leaves us to grapple with the contradiction that explodes when we bring them together. One is close to being ridiculous by daring to pair certain words, certain superimpositions of phantasms. And one runs the risk of thinking too early that here starts the obligation of silence. Yet, one should be stubborn and endeavor to delay it. We know quite well, that in the long run we will have to be silent. But not before we will have exhausted the resources of language, including poetry. No one can boast, when he gives up talk, that he is protected against the alternate partialities which were the price of his discourse. God All Other, and God in me more me than me. God whom I seek and who seeks me. Inexpressible God, expressed in the Bible. Tender God, severe God. Strong God, weak God. God the source of all joy, God in desolation. Sensible God, God Spirit.

One reads at times very beautiful pages about God, his attributes, his greatness, his mystery. One would willingly call them mystical if there was not a caution against cheapening the word. But if the name of Jesus Christ is missing, suspicion cannot be avoided. How does the author know what he is saying? Where did he find it? The Christians are right to suspect theological talk which does not proceed from the knowledge of Christ, or which unfolds without explicit references to his Gospel. One must never get tired of repeating the key sentence read in Saint John: "Who has seen me has seen the Father" (Jn 14:9). It means that the unity of God and man in Jesus is a temporal manifestation of the eternal unity of the Father and the Son in the Holy Spirit. The voice of the Son is the voice of the Father. To hear Jesus is to hear the Father.

Hans Urs von Balthasar suggests an excellent image: the believer—he says—hears this voice "as if stereophonically."[53]

Nowhere outside of Christianity do the divine truth and the spiritual quest coincide fully in the objective presence of a historical man. In Christianity God is what Christ says, shows, and does. An intimate knowledge of the suffering of Jesus must therefore come before theological reflection on the suffering of God. One must first read the Gospel like a child. But with a great deal of love. Only love can lead the ear and the eye to the point where, gestures and words having been left behind, one touches the soul that brought them forth. The Holy Spirit is the Spirit of the Father as he is the Spirit of the Son, and could he not also be granted to the shudders of the human flesh and heart of the Word? Jesus thrilled with joy, but, as the *Imitation* puts it: "His whole life was cross and martyrdom" (11:12, 7); and Saint Ignatius of Loyola evokes: "the pains, travails and suffering that Christ had to bear from the moment of his birth to the mystery of his passion."[54]

Rather than contemplate Jesus exterior to myself, *before* me, I must enter into him in order to turn with him toward the Father and toward men. Thus will I feel more intensely what he feels when he meets with coldness or bad faith; when he measures the distance between the sublimity of the human vocation and the miserable use that many have for their freedom; when he sees—as Claudel puts it—the "sabotage" of this "intention toward the heights that is in us" and which God ceaselessly brings to the center of the souls when creating them. The presence and attention of Jesus to man at variance with himself are a participation. To know is to be part of. He does not look at me, he touches me. He coincides. It is within himself that he hears how painfully things creak inside of me. And whatever be the "dark complicity" of misery and sin, there is the immense realm of suffering symbolized in the language of poets by the stoned bird and the blasted tree: illness, mourning, infirmity, failure, loneliness.

Jesus walks all over this realm. "He spends his life in the most painful areas of our humanity."[55] And this too creaks in his heart. He calls himself a physician, he wants to be a physician. He calls himself and wants to be an advocate. He is both. The good physician is compassionate, and in an emergency he rushes, saying: "I am coming right away." (The use of "right away"—*statim*—is frequent in the Gospel). He has only one goal: to heal. Jesus heals massively, without choosing: "And those who were suffering from diseases and painful complaints of one kind or another . . . were all (*omnes*) brought to him, and he cured them" (Mt 4:24). But he is pierced by a thorn when unbelief prevents him from working any miracle in Nazareth (Mk 6:5). The good advocate counsels, helps, assists, encourages. He is not a pure technician of the law. He also participates, all the more closely that he knows his client more intimately. Jesus knows "what man has in him" (Jn 2:25), and he knows that God knows: "Whatever accusations [our conscience] may raise against us, . . . God is greater than our conscience and he knows everything" (1 Jn 3:20). No part of the file is irrelevant to him. Far from looking at things with the rigidity of the law, a word is enough for his plea: "It is your son, it is your daughter," he tells the Father. Nothing more. How could he not be hurt when suspicion sprouts and grows before him, and when instead of "taking refuge" in his weakness, the multitudes insist on "relying on princes"? (Ps 118:9)

We read that when the prodigal son came back, the father was "moved with pity" (Lk 15:20). This is a weak translation of the Greek *esplagknisthe* which evokes a turmoil of entrails. This is not a skin-deep emotion but an upheaval of the being in its depth, the call of the blood. The joy of the father is not coming out of indifference, as an event breaking for a moment the banality of the days, but out of a mortal fear that is reduced to ashes at last. "My son was lost and he is found."

"Far from feeling the slightest weakness with regard to sin, far from thinking to minimize its seriousness, to soften its ravages, Jesus, on the contrary, sees it in its sinister depth: death, perdition. And to make us understand what this perdition is, what is irretrievable in it and what this irretrievability means for God who knows its risk and runs it, Jesus evokes one of the most banal and painful human experiences. To lose something which is important to us, even if the object has very little real value, a simple bill: it is always a cruel blow, it is the sign of the failure that saps everything we do and threatens all that we love. And, Jesus tells us, God himself has had this experience. The joy he feels when he forgives, the emotion sweeping over him when he recovers his children, is the emotion of one who already saw what he loved being destroyed, and who still shudders when he thinks of what could have happened if he had not been able to catch up with them."[56]

Why, when I read *Epaves* (Wrecks) by Julien Green, am I suddenly taken to the very heart of the Gospel? "The woman had stopped between two trees . . . In her, misery added so much to old age, that it was impossible to say how old she was; yet, she retained an unexplainable remnant of vanity often seen in very aged people whose head gets confused, and her hair of a greenish gray hue peeped from under a black toque on which trembled a feather. Her small stature was bent as if she had been carrying a man on her back; she was dressed in blue and black rags and had slippers on her feet which she dragged on the stones without ever lifting them . . . that sad body had had its youth."[57] It was impossible for Jesus not to meet such wrecks on the squares or in the narrow streets of Jerusalem. He saw and touched sad bodies. If the sensitivity of a novelist is touched by the distress of old and ravaged flesh— *sarx palaia*—as Aeschylus said—how much more Jesus' sensitivity! He is not only the God of our glorious times, but of our whole history. The genesis of man is his joy, but he is not like a marble statue before the cruel phases of his begetting us to Life. Our decrepitudes also make him shudder.

At the gates of Nain, Jesus "felt sorry"—again the word *esplagknisthe*—at the sorrow of a widow whose only son was going to be buried. He says "Do not cry," and immediately brings the young man back to life (Lk 7:11-15). But at the tomb of Lazarus, he weeps when he sees Mary and the Jews with her weeping. Why these tears? asks Newman.[58] Spontaneous tenderness of the friend, horror of the "breath of the tomb" which will engulf Lazarus again in the future: the miracle is that of a "respite, not a resurrection." There is more: God himself is facing his own death here. "The disciples of Jesus wanted to dissuade him from going to Judea lest the Jews kill him. Their fear was confirmed. He came to bring Lazarus back to life, and the renown of that miracle was the immediate cause of his arrest and crucifixion . . . He felt that Lazarus woke up to life in virtue of his own sacrifice, that he was going down into the very tomb from which Lazarus came up." The tears of Jesus are the beginning of his agony; they express the simple reaction of his sensitivity in front of human death. At least we are permitted to think so together with the great Newman.

If there were no suffering of the Father, would we have to think that the Son testifies to a greater love? But, according to Saint John, the Father and the Son are one (10:30); the Father and the Son work together (5:17); what belongs to the Son is of the Father (16:15; 17:10); the Son is in the Father and the Father is in the Son (14:11). If no one "can have a greater love than to lay down his life for his friends" (15:13), it is from the Father, whose Image he is, that the Son receives this love which includes the gift of life. To give one's life is the very act of the Power of the Father, coming from the fullness of love. "God did not spare his own Son but gave him up to benefit us all," says Saint Paul (Rm 8:32). And about fifty years later, Saint John: "God loved the world so much that he gave his only Son" (Jn 3:16). There is no ambiguity in the words: to give, to give up. One cannot believe that the two apostles and theologians imagine a coldly accepted gift and giving up. The truth of God is rather offered to them as the paroxysm of a heartbreak. They hear as it were, a flashing cry within the heart of the Trinity. For "compassion is not a tepid gift of a surplus thing, it is a passion"[59] in the two meanings of the word.

Men will not be given a more perfect image of God, *such as he is in himself*, than the man Jesus agonizing, insulted, crucified. Shortly before dying, he cried: "My God, why have you forsaken me?" (Mk 15:34; Mt 27:46). It is the beginning of Psalm 22, which expresses at the same time anguish and trust. Trust having vanquished anguish. The suffering of Jesus, at the supreme hour, ceases to be a suffering in communion. He does not know anymore that the Father is suffering with him. He suffers alone, therefore more. This is the limit. I dare think here about the distress of a woman who would not know that her husband suffers as much as she does from the death of their child. For Christ, it is the bottomless abyss of *kenosis*, out of which emerges a confidence based only on itself and therefore tremendous. It is, in the deprivation of communion, the most intimate communion. The Spirit is the bond. In the Encyclical *Miserentissimus*, Pius XI, that strong man, begged men to console God. He added, quoting Saint Augustine: "Give me someone who loves, and he will understand what I am saying."

Chapter Six

REFLECTION

The believer daring enough to evoke, even in a questioning manner, the possibility of a suffering God, seems to go beyond the limits of provocation. Reason, already shocked at the idea of a God who becomes man, is overwhelmed as if by an offending challenge. The essential attributes of the Being are in question: he is perfect, eternal, immutable, unchangeable, invulnerable. To deny from the outset that one could believe in a suffering God is a common temptation, especially if one remembers that, as early as at the beginning of the IIIrd century, Saint Hippolytus and Tertullian had to fight against the Patripassianists who admitted the existence of a "passion" of the Father. In truth, Patripassianism was a form of modalism: the Word being only another name of the Father, it was the Father who became incarnate and suffered. The question we are asking has nothing to do with that heresy. Far from all the trinitarian and christological controversies, the word, more than its contents, speaks today to the imagination and impels more than one person to a systematic recoil.

The other temptation is that of fideism, which refuses a dialogue between faith and philosophy. The mystery of God's suffering is a specific—and paroxysmal—point of an irreducible antinomy. The veto of reason will not prevent a fideist from relying without critique on the Bible. His choice is made: the

God of Abraham, Isaac, Jacob and Jesus Christ is not and cannot be the God of the philosophers and the scientists. Is fideism "the ultimate trick of selfishness in which man worships nothing else but his emotions"?[60] Is it a concession made to popular sensitivity with which one feels a vague solidarity? Is it, after the great shock-wave of conversion, a spontaneous aversion to discourse, as if one measured all of a sudden and forever the immeasurable distance between the wise man and God? Is it the effect of a sympathy dictated by choice for Pascal or Kierkegaard, whose thoughts can easily be exaggerated according to one's own inclinations? Is it, quite simply, a laziness of the spirit? There is fideism and fideism. But there is no room for any fideism in the Church. It is always—sooner or later, and the Church knows this—the grave-digger of faith. Therefore the Fathers of the first Christian centuries had the constant concern, while retaining the transcendence of mystery, to supply answers to the demands of reason, God's daughter. They knew that a religion, when it is no more than a life-style, is sentenced to a progressive degradation which ends in disappearance. The word *truth* had a meaning for them. They did not sacrifice to usefulness, even spiritual usefulness. For "God is Spirit" (Jn 4:24).

At the dawn of Greek thought, Xenophanes had launched the motion of intelligence towards a severe criticism of the human forms in which his compatriots wrapped the gods. He blazed the trail for the great Eleatics, Parmenides and Zeno. Unable to attain to the concept of a personal God having created man in his image, those philosophers at least contested vigorously a God made in the image of man. The criticism of religious anthropomorphisms was in the West the beginning of reflective thought. The fundamental dogma is the immobility of the Being. The Being is; he is All. He is All there is. He cannot cease to be. He cannot cease having been. He cannot cease being. There is neither original nor terminal nothingness. If all is, nothing becomes. Motion is only a semblance. "Noon up there. Noon without motion."[61]

At the extreme opposite is Heraclitus of Ephesus, for whom everything is moving and changing. The being becomes. One only has to question nature, that of things and that of men, to perceive in it a ceaseless mutation, a game of opposites begetting and destroying each other. The primordial fire will finally absorb all forms: "I smell here my own smoke."[62]

The philosophy of the following centuries disdained the Ephesian. It purified from its sketchy pantheism the Eleatic conception and reconquered against it the distinction between man and god. But what Parmenides affirmed of the All, that philosophy never ceased—Idea of Plato, Prime Mover of Aristotle, the One of Plotinus—to attribute it to the Being.

There was in Heraclitus a kernel of tragedy, a seed of anxiety, a threat of skepticism, a worrisome darkness. "His way," writes Char, "leads to the somber and flashing stage of our days."[63] Our contemporaries have dug out Heraclitus, just as they have brought about a sympathy for Qoheleth. But the straight path of *philosophia perennis* unfolded in the West according to the sure logic of the principle of identity, protected against contradictions, metamorphoses and fluidities: if God is eternal, he is immutable; if he is immutable, he is impassible. The Christian apologists did not believe that they had to reject these concepts. Yet they believed in a becoming-man of God. A becoming? No, God does not become: he is. But Scripture testifies that he is Love and Freedom. Christ who is true man is also true God. How can one deny that, out of love, God freely *becomes*? Unless one thinks like the Docetists that he *appears* as man in Jesus, though he *is not* so. In such a case God would be cheating. In order to save his transcendence, one casts aspersions on his honesty. The Church refused the easy solution which wounds love, and for three centuries fought against all odds to maintain in the Man-God the divinity of man and the humanity of God. The dogmatic cathedral is "at the same time immovable and in motion with all its pillars from the door to the choir."[64] In motion, for there is a development of dogma; immovable for, in spite of controversies, the immutability of God is never on the line. Yet Origen wrote:

"The Savior came down to earth out of pity for the human race. He suffered our passions before suffering on the cross, even before he condescended to take on our flesh: for if he had not suffered them first, he would not have come to participate in our human life. What is this passion that he first suffered for us? It is the passion of love. But the Father himself, God of the universe, he who is full of forbearance, of mercy and pity, does he not also suffer in some way? Or do you remain ignorant of the fact that, when he deals with human matters, he suffers a human passion? 'For Yahweh carried you as a man carries his child' (Dt 1:31). God thus takes our ways on himself as the Son of God takes on our passions. The Father himself is not impassible! If we pray to him, he has pity and compassion. He suffers a passion of love."[65]

Father de Lubac comments: "Surprising and admirable text! Origen knows how susceptible the philosophers are on this point. He himself has learnedly enunciated the dogma of divine impassibility in another text. Even here, one feels that he is controlling his style, and that he is aware of his daring . . . (But) he accepts, he chooses, he brings forth the paradoxical expression: 'the Father himself is not impassible!' Undoubtedly he is very far from . . . any vulgar pathos. But against a reasonable timidity which is too concerned with the opinion of the wise people of this world, he affirms that in his love for man, the Impassible has suffered a passion of mercy."[66] At the time of Origen, the word *pathe*—not only in the meaning of suffering, but more broadly of passion, emotion—had in the language of the philosophers a pejorative connotation. It evoked most of the time, a physical or metaphysical deficiency and a moral degradation. This is why, in spite of the evangelical testimony, one often hesitated to use it, even when it came to Christ.

If Origen dares adopt it when talking about the Father, it is because he transforms its meaning very deeply: it means to him nothing else than the suffering of loving, in the heart of fullness. The most admirable thing about his text is that he firmly maintains the Father-Son duality, and at the same time rejects an opposition which he fears will finally lead to the refusal of the Father. It is known that, against all genuinely Christian tradition, this movement of refusal is dangerously accelerated today. In a little book written as a dialogue—*De passibili et impassibili in Deo* (Passibility and Impassibility in God)—Gregory the Thaumaturge, a disciple of Origen, attempts to reconcile the impassibility of God, which he refuses to question—"How could it be possible for us not to confess that God is impassible?"—with the suffering love in Jesus Christ. It is in the Passion itself, he says, and in the death of the Son that the immutability of the divine essence is manifested. Just as the salamander has enough cold in itself to cool the flame surrounding it and not be burnt by it, God yields to death and remains incorruptible. He commiserates without sustaining a loss.

Saint Bernard will put a stronger emphasis on the mercy to which Scripture testifies: "If God is impassible, he is not devoid of compassion, since nothing is more inherent to him than pity and pardon. Those who are united to the God of mercy must therefore be merciful even if they are far from all misery: delivered from suffering, they commiserate with it."67 Already Clement of Alexandria, very firm on the subject of divine *apatheia*, had "expressly reserved the rights of mercy (*eleos*). He understood quite well that it could not be excluded from Christian perfection; but not daring to openly contradict

Stoic orthodoxy, he found a distinction that saved the day. Passion, as he pointed out, includes an element of sensible pain: but mercy is not the same as pain; therefore it is not a passion, and then nothing prevents the perfect One from knowing it."[68] Saint Thomas, facing the same difficulty, proposes a similar distinction: "Mercy is sovereignly attributable to God, but according to the effect it produces, not according to the suffered passion—*secundum effectum, non secundum passionis affectum.* In fact, one is called merciful because he suffers from the misery of another one as if it were his very own. He then endeavors to cure it: which is the effect of mercy. To be saddened by the misery of another does not suit God, but to repel this misery, namely what is lacking in another, this suits him to a supreme degree."[69] Thus the dogma of God's impassibility survives in the Middle Ages, without any solution in continuity with the patristic era.

Yet, Jacques Maritain confesses here that he is embarrassed. What Saint Thomas affirms "is perfectly true," he says, "and it is quite clear that sadness and affliction, because they imply in themselves dependence and imperfection, could not be attributed to God. Yet, this leaves the mind unsatisfied, especially when it remembers" the Gospel parables of the lost sheep and the prodigal son, the sinning woman of Luke 7:36-50 the Samaritan woman, and the adulterous woman. Not only what Jesus *does*, the Father *does* too; but what Jesus *is*, so *is* the Father. Then Maritain positively contradicts Saint Thomas: "If a perfection such as love, to which mercy is so close, is properly attributed to God, it is not only because of the effect that is produced. Love is not only credited to God because he is the cause of good in the beings. Love, not only in what it *does*, but in what it *is* is a perfection of God and is God himself. Is it not the same with mercy? It is in God according to what it *is* and not only according to what it *does*, but in a state of perfection *for which there is no name.*" Faithful to the rule of analogy, Maritain admits that there is in God "*something unnamed and unnameable*, properly unknowable through any of our concepts . . . a splendor . . . to which corresponds, not only as to its effect, but also as to its essence, what mercy is in us."

Far from the *pathe* of a degrading kind, all that is noble and majestic in human suffering must have its "eternal pattern" in the heart of the Creator, and be an integral part of his beatitude. "Perfect peace, yet infinitely exulting above the humanly conceivable and burning in its flames what is for us apparently irreconcilable." However, it remains evident that this beatitude is "absolutely immutable."[70] Naive and profound, old Arkel exclaims in *Pelléas*: "If I were God, I would have pity for the heart of men." "There was in Paris," writes Julien Green, "a writer who called on the telephone to tell me [quoting this sentence] that it was 'blasphemous'."[71] The theme of *compassion without passion* was taken up again at the time of Modernism by Baron von Hügel. To sympathize actively is not necessarily to suffer, he said. "Father Damien did not have to be a leper to love the lepers. He understood them and commiserated with their suffering better than the lepers knew how to do it ordinarily among themselves. The riches of his imagination and the promptitude of his sensitivity replaced very well his lack of personal experience. How much more God must penetrate the concerns of his creatures without losing his divine perfection!"

It is true that suffering does not always precede sympathy, but is it not its necessary consequence, at least if one takes seriously upon oneself the unhappiness of the others? Certainly, but compassion is in itself an act distinct from sensible trauma ("physiological shock," "nervous perturbation"), which is the rebound it has in the carnal creature. What occurs in man does not occur in God who is a spiritual being.[72]

Commenting on this, Maurice Nédoncelle questions himself: "Some thinkers deprive God of all emotional life. They deem that feeling is the awareness of an organic trauma, and that God cannot be so affected since he is purely spiritual. Their argumentation is based on a summary psychology of affective states in human experience. And above all, the transposition made to divine things is quite hasty. Why should one refuse to place in God an immense life of feeling, when one does not hesitate to credit him with an immense life of intelligence? If human emotion is tied to corporeal conditions, it is also true for human thought; and if in spite of this material link, human thought seems to us a participation in God, why should it be otherwise for our best sensitivity?"

In *La réciprocite des consciences*[73] (Reciprocity of consciousnesses) the philosopher of Strasbourg (Nédoncelle) notes that "unfortunately the phenomenology of fine sensitivity has never been attempted: we are totally at a loss for words to describe the nuances of our mind. In any event one thing is certain: this land will not remain unexplored; the religious demands of our contemporaries reject totally any verbal answer that would be given on these points." "The philosophy of Revelation," Schelling had already said, "is not for the seated and satisfied, but for those who are hungry and thirsty for a real, radical regeneration of their way of thinking."[74]

"God is not expressed by motion, but even less by immobility."[75] If there is an anthropomorphism in saying that God suffers, there is a greater one in thinking that he does not suffer. The concept of a passible God is perhaps a scandal for reason, but the reality of an impassible God is repugnant to the heart which has its own reasons. The impassibility of God is deduced from the perfection of his nature, but any nature is imperfect if it has to be captive to what it is. Marble also is impassible: it is captive to its coldness and opacity.

The God of Aristotle was captive, in the name of the perfection of his nature, to the necessity of ignoring the very existence of the imperfect world. In Valéry's poem, Sémiramis tells herself: "Your imperial eye thirsts for the great empire which, under your hard scepter, must endure happiness,"[76] but nations moan under duress, even duress to happiness, at least if they have a taste for freedom. God is not the dupe of such a necessity. God chooses himself: he is not what he is, he is what he wants to be. There are passions without greatness; there is no greatness without passion. To cross out with a thick and strong stroke of the pen the metaphysics of divine impassibility according to their entire Greek, patristic and medieval extension, is a modern temptation. There is no guarantee that such an operation is without danger. If it is permitted on this precise point to regret a certain unilateralism of former centuries, at least in the West, it would be an uncertain progress to impose a contrary unilateralism.

The diversity of symbols protects us against the risks of sectarianism, systematicism, and idolatry. Blondel knew it: "Which is why he recommended as a game, a kind of diversifying freedom in the use of symbols and concepts. He advised his friend von Hügel, whose personalism was excessive—he would have given the opposite advice to an Aristotelian—to balance somehow the notion of person applied to God by that of substance."[77] Thus one will guard against eliminating the concept of nature or of essence: because God is not captive to his nature, it does not mean that he has no nature. Neither will one doubt the sovereign independence of God: God is not God if he is said to depend on the world.

To eliminate certain fantastic interpretations of Teilhard, Father Martelet stresses: "Is not God immutable? Immutable, says the Bible, is his fidelity! How can one say that God changes? Was he not God before creation? Would he be more so, or on the contrary would he cease to be so, since the Incarnation? In fact, if Teilhard were saying that it is the creation of the world that makes God's existence possible, it would be an error. Far from it being the life of the world which

6

makes the Life of God, it is on the Life of God that the existence of the world is based and established, for he alone is in himself and by himself the Principle and eternal Source of being. If Teilhard, passing from the creative act to the mystery of Christ, meant to say that God is the Trinitarian God of Revelation only because he becomes incarnate and that before becoming man he would not yet be himself, the doctrine of God's immortality would be opposed to the idea of Teilhard. ... God being immutable means, for Teilhard as for any other believer, that God does not owe his being Son and Spirit to the fact of his Incarnation, but to the fact that he is." Though, a few lines further: "However, Teilhard deems that this affirmation of divine immutability understood in such a way *neutralizes* errors, but that it does not yet express the whole truth. The most paradoxical is that God, the true God, must be defined *in himself* and *for us* through a passage to the other, and as such, by a true becoming of love. . . . God is immutable God only by being, as Father, an eternal *passage* to the otherness of his Son in the Unity of the Spirit."[78]

Gregory Palamas, in the XIVth century—and all the tradition of Eastern Christianity until Bulgakov—distinguishes in God *essence* or *superessence* which is inaccessible, and the participable *energies*. If the divine being were totally identified with his essence, God could not go out of himself to act outside of himself: creation would be impossible. But "if essence is necessarily being, being is not necessarily essence." Hence God can manifest himself in his very being, while remaining impartible in his essence. His will, not his essence, is at the origin of created things. Creation leaves his essence immutable: God has no need of creation and his power is subjected to no limit, for such a need and such a limit would be at the same time weakness and "complexity." If God were only essence, he could not be at the same time free, immutable and active; if he, himself, were not "essence and energy" he could not possess *naturally* the creative power and *begin* to create. "How," Palamas asks, "could the many divine thoughts and the images of the beings to come reflected in these thoughts . . . be in themselves essence? Through them, indeed, God is related to the beings; while through essence, he is outside all relativity."[79]

"Essence and energies are therefore, in a certain way," Olivier Clément says, "antinomic vitalities of the absolute Living One who gives himself absolutely while always remaining other . . . The distinction between essence and energies is an extension of the great trinitarian antinomy of essence and hypostases, source of all communion . . . " (The mystery of the Trinity "suggests absolute coincidence, in the living God, of identity and difference") Thus God can "come out of his inaccessibility, of his immutability, to go to the extreme of sacrificial love."[80] "The last presupposition of kenosis," Urs von Balthasar says on the other hand, "is 'forgetfulness of self' of the persons (as pure relations) in the intratrinitarian life of love . . . (there is) a lasting supra-temporal state of the Lamb, not only such as the French School presented it, but as a continuation of a 'sacrificial state' of the resurrected one, though as a state of the Son coextensive with all creation and thus affecting somehow his divine being."[81]

"Hegel," Karl Barth said, "is the great tentativeness and the great temptation." Tentativeness: to overcome the opposition of reason and history, integrate tragedy into logic, the real suffering of history into the ideal necessity of the spirit. Temptation: to squeeze events, especially the event of Jesus, in the vise of the system; to stifle divine freedom in a cage of necessity. Theologians are divided today on the question of knowing whether tentativeness can be pursued outside of temptation. The swollen shadow of the philosopher covers many books, at times making them heavier, at times stimulating them. The ones as well the others should stop shaking: either for fear of seeming to give a victory to an enterprise of secularization of the Christian faith, or—conversely—for fear of seeming too lukewarm with regard to one of the greatest names of modern times. A Christian must be able to question himself about the suffering of God without transposing Hegel, which does not mean that he has to ignore what he owes him.

The word *becoming* belongs, must belong to the vocabulary of Christology. It is vain to attempt avoiding it, let alone eliminating it. "The Word was made flesh" (Jn 1:14) means that God *became* man. Could that have happened without any change in him? If we say with Saint Thomas, leaning on his distinction between "real relation" and "relation of reason,"[82] that the change is entirely on the side of man, not at all on the side of God, we might rescue the Being, but we would also wound Love. Our painful history would not really be, in Jesus Christ, the history of the Word, our becoming his becoming, our life his life. The event of the Incarnation would be an event for man, not for God. Péguy denounced the sham of those who see the Incarnation only "from the side of eternity." He was right. It is not only, he said, "a story that happened ... to God." One needs "the counterpart, the countersight, as it were": the earth by "greeting eternity," "gave birth to God." The Incarnation "is in the order of temporal events as a flower and a temporal fruit ... as an achievement, as a temporal crowning, a supreme feat of temporal fecundity ... a carnal implantation ... a fructification at the summit ... a story ... which happened to the earth." There is "a carnal begetting" of God, and it went "through crimes of the flesh." *Ex ea quae fuit Uriae*: "honest Matthew does not hide" of whom Solomon was the son.[83]

But there is an equal risk of sham if we recoil before the words *becoming* and *change* for fear of wounding divine immutability, and we establish a new Docetism, more subtle than the old one, but just as suspicious. The Incarnation is not only, in Jesus Christ, a change *of* man, it is a change, in Jesus Christ, of God *in* man. It is, as Péguy said, "the maximum of man, and so to speak, the maximum of God." There is a maximum of God only if there is a maximum of love. There is no maximum of love if "all the becoming, all history with its travails, remains on this side of the absolute abyss separating, without confusion, the immutable and necessary God from the sensible and contingent world."[84]

Reflection on the mystery of God is not content with merely enunciating at the same time his Trinity and his Unity. It digs deeper, to the point where Trinity appears as perfection of Unity: if God were not a Trinity, his Unity would not be one of fullness but one of flat identity. In the same way, the mind is not satisfied when we affirm simultaneously that God is immutable in himself and mutable in the other. God is not a Sphinx; neither is man a "guesser of enigmas." Obscure in itself, mystery enlightens. It must therefore be possible, if not to understand, at least to have a foreboding—foreboding is not alien to concrete experience or to intelligence—that in God becoming is the perfection of the being, motion the perfection of immobility, change the perfection of immutability. But in the kingdom of love—God is Love (1 Jn 4:8, 16)—the meaning of these words is radically transfigured.

Immobile eternity, such as more than one *imagines*, is not fascinating even if based on happiness and love. The phantasm of boredom erases all attraction. There are, in literature, passages without flaw that can put us to sleep. Julien Green talks about "the boring perfection" of certain pages in Mérimée: "This elegant tone, this perfect mastery of his emotions, this distrust of any impulse, this brilliant and icy sentence . . ."[85] The charming Jules Laforgue entertains himself by evoking "celestial Eternullity."[86] On a graver mode, the head of John the Baptist, in Mallarmé's poem chooses to remain terrestrial after his execution rather than risk a "haggard leap" towards "eternal cold."[87] As we see in the movies frozen motions—sports games, horse races—one imagines

God as a complex of petrified impulses: outstretched arms of the Father towards the Son and of the Son towards the Father, and their mutual kiss, the Spirit. Immobilized life: could it still be Life?

If we cannot avoid anthropomorphism, it is better when we evoke eternity, to lean on the experience of novelty than on that of repetition. The eternity of man is youth, wonder, desire. "Unquenchable surfeit," said Saint Augustine. If the eternity of God were not in itself a bubbling spring, a rushing cascade, and the freshness of love, it would only offer us a participation in a monotonous duration.

Le Senne once expressed surprise at the fact that one could consider eternal life as "a final state": "There is no final state," he said. "We must set aside the doctrines which make of time a passage through which the mind would be introduced into a state of fullness out of which it could not fall down." Father de Montcheuil replied: "If there is no final state, is it impossible that there be a perfect act? Genuine eternal life in Christianity does not lead to a freezing of the soul in the passive contemplation of an object, were it the most perfect of all. If the perfection of any spirit is the triumph of charity in it, and if God is persistent Charity, the achievement of the spirit is to become a participant in this immanent activity of God. It is not a fall into immobility and inertia, pleasure replacing effort: it is the perfection of activity replacing its imperfect exercise."[88] To put things in another way, man does not cease being historical. God is never a perfect object for him. To deny that God could be an object is to deny at the same time that our history could end. It continues, totally different, infinitely happy, in the dynamics of an unlimited desire.[89] *Vita mutatur, non tollitur.*

If desire were to cease with God
Ah, I would envy Hell for keeping it![90]

At the end of his life, Jacques Maritain dedicated to the Little Brothers of Jesus, with whom he lived in Toulouse, a page which is not naive but candid and simple, out of which he excluded the *quo* and the *quod*, less imaginative and more rational than it seems at first, and which might have delighted Therese of Lisieux. I glean a few sentences: "As the incarnate Word had on this earth a life that was both human and divine, in the same manner the blessed in Heaven have entered divine life itself through vision, but they also lead, outside of vision though penetrated by its radiance, a glorious and transfigured human life. There is between them . . . intellectual communication (wordless of course) depending on the free will of each one of them. Every blessed is master of the thoughts of his heart and shares them freely with whomever he chooses . . . in Heaven there are *events* that happen: new blessed ones arrive, arrive continuously from earth to be born to life eternal; they are welcomed by the others, friendships are founded . . . All this makes for quite a history, in a duration which is different from that of our own history . . . the love that the saints had on earth for those they loved, is kept in Heaven, transfigured, not abolished by glory. You remember the words of Saint Therese of Lisieux: 'I want to spend my Heaven doing good on earth.' It goes very far, in what we could call the humanism of the saints even in Heaven . . . Why am I telling you about those we have known in person? It is because there is a special role to be credited to the chosen who cannot be canonized, the unseen saints. . . . They brought to Heaven the memory of their friends. They continue loving them as they loved them . . ." This is the extreme opposite of the "eternal cold."

When I hear the Song of the dead children—*Kindertoten-lieder*—of Mahler, a prayer springs spontaneously in me as if each one of these notes, so pure, poignant and joyful, were evoking a vision turning into a prayer. As a priest "who rejoices with those who rejoice and is sad with those in sorrow" (Rm

12:15), I could be the father, or the husband, or the lover, the music could be more or less the same as the words of Rückert with which I start to pray: "A little lamp went out under my tent, glory to the Sun, light of the world!"

You are now younger and younger every day, and every day more and more mature in the serious enthusiasm of a spiritual intelligence more and more detached every day. Reasonable enthusiasm was for Rimbaud the song of the angels! Seriousness, not of austerity, but sovereignly calm! You are, in your luminous flesh, more passionately in love than you ever were.

This radiant smile starting like the song of a bird that delighted me until I blushed, is reflecting today all the sparkle of God. Your desire is possession and your possession desire. There is in you fullness and continuous increase of fullness. With the same impulse, you go to God and to me who loves you. You are deeper and deeper in the heart of God and in my heart. Mine, but not apart from other men, our brothers, for if I were the only object of your attention, you could not contemplate God any more! You are a certain hue of blue, unique, irreplaceable, in a great stained glass window composed of billions of colors. I have contributed to the making of this blue which is you: there is something of me in it. I myself am this hue, not identical but similar to yours, now opaque and covered with this dust called *glutinum* by Saint Augustine. God and you with him (for the saints intercede, and to intercede is to act) continuously breathe on it. The same Breath creates and cleanses.

Purgatory, in which I firmly believe, as I firmly believe in all the dogmas of my Church, started in you, in the painful passage over a treshold, passage to a youthfulness which will never end. I feel an impulse quickening in you, the power and the sweetness of an embrace. Any embrace is sweetness and power. Sweetness and power in you—alas not in me!—grow together. All the immensity of the cosmos is enclosed for you in the warmest intimacy, which for your spiritual eyes, grows and deepens in your heart. To know—no, to believe, to believe and feel—to what extent you are happy, would make me cry for joy! I would like, as a father who has lost my little girl already grown into a young lady, as a husband who has buried the mortal body of my wife, not to have any other joy but your own. At least, I want to need your joy!

Prayer, it is true, does not dry my tears. They flow while Mahler sings. Suffering and joy can thus coexist. In us, at least. But in God?

One would have to deny that God suffers if *all* suffering were partially the effect of a frustrated selfishness. This selfishness is immanent to human love, even a very pure one: to weep for the other who is no more where I am, is also to weep for myself. Nothing in man is absolutely pure. The child himself is the symbol of a purity toward which we should never cease to strive, but that we know we will never attain, even at the last agony. Otherwise, the Catholic belief in Purgatory would have no meaning. Can one conceive of a pure suffering, interior to love which is only love? If one can do this, it is the suffering of God. "To love," Jean Lacroix says, "is to promise and to promise oneself never to use towards the beloved the means of power. And to refuse all power is to expose oneself to refusal, incomprehension, and unfaithfulness."[91] There are multiple "powers," from seduction which looks innocent, up to the most abject violence. Between one and the other, there are all the twistings of genuine values, such as benefaction and sacrifice. We know well enough that vanity, flattery, even lie, are worms hidden in the beautiful fruits we offer.

To accept these hidden "rapes," is to love poorly. The only language suited to love is prayer. God does not "want"; he "prays."[92] To want implies power. To pray is to give up power. It is asking in fear and hope: will my wish be fulfilled? Will it not? In a united family, people pray for each other: they show what they desire. When it comes to God, the word "will" is traditional, and Jesus himself adopted it: it is at the heart of the *Our Father*. But we must guard against giving it a meaning incompatible with love. The same goes for the word "commandment." If man must pray to God, it is because God is the first in praying to man. "He loved us first" (1 Jn 4:10); he was the first one to tell us his desire and to address a prayer to us: what I offer you—Myself—do you want to accept it? When man fulfills God, he reaches the highest level of existence.

It is a fallacy to think that perfect love can ignore a need for reciprocity. When God invites us to love him in return, it is not because he curls or folds back on himself: it is—love being the supreme value—because he desires us to live in him as he lives in himself. Disinterestedness pushed to the limit is no more than indifference to the other. Pretending to go beyond self, one denies self. To have an idea of the risk God runs in creating, and how the desire for reciprocity, hence also hope and fear, are not alien to his love for man, we must first contemplate, such as it is in itself, the perfect trinitarian Charity.

Richard of Saint-Victor directs and guides our look in the best way. In brief, this is what he says: One must take the viewpoint of love itself, and not of happiness, in order to understand that something would be missing from the one who loves in a sovereign way if the sovereignly loved person were not also sovereignly loving. For only the perfection of love is worthy of being loved perfectly. Sovereignly loving and sovereignly loved, this means that each of the divine Persons, being perfect in love, is sovereignly lovable. Perfection of love could not be without perfection of reciprocity.[93] The creature being finite and sinful, is not sovereignly lovable. What *is* in the intratrinitarian love, God cannot refuse to desire it to *become*, through Christ, in his *life-with* man, always more, eternally more, as Péguy would put it. Since he cannot refuse to desire, unless he did not love, how could God, as long as we are *in via*, not *fear* our refusal, a lack of reciprocity of love, or its weakness? Fear is the opposite of hope. As he loves and prays first, God is also the first to hope and fear.

I transcribe here a page of Pierre Lachièze-Rey, a philosopher whose thinking is rigorous:

If the divine consciousness and personality are the conditions of all destinies, it is only insofar as the *relationships between God and the human personalities take on the most perfect form that we could conceive and in the making of which we could succeed, under the very impulsion of our mind as a guided power.* And this perfect form is neither that of authority and fear nor that of cooperation in domination and power; it can be conceived only as a reciprocity of Love: ascending love in man, love made of confidence, abandoning himself to receive God in his intelligence, his sensitivity and his will—descending love in God who gives himself and in so doing moves man to a growing possession of his being, insofar as man accepts to greet him freely.

In deepening this idea of *reciprocity of the gift* in its two different forms, ascending and descending, in not translating it simply into a verbal formula, but in entering into its design and movement, the philosophical soul will go from discovery to discovery without even being able to exhaust the riches, because confidence and gift can be infinitely developed; but it will find in it a special condemnation, new and final, of Wisdom. The latter has never known *charity*; it even rejected it as a weakness and pretended to replace it with a certain virtue of *generosity* similar to the light of the sun which lights up spaces through a simple manifestation of its nature; thus the wisdom of a wise man would radiate on the rest of mankind without his losing his Olympian serenity, and without his putting himself at the mercy of fools. But such an attitude would not correspond to true love; the latter is not *giving*, but *self-giving*, and the giving of self always implies a *risk*, that of lack of response, lack of welcome, that of rejection and denial.

It remains true that Brunschvicg, in *le Progrès de la Conscience* (Progress of Conscience), thought that he could go back to the concept of Stoic *autarkeia* without renouncing love; he denounced what he called "anguish of reciprocity" as a stage to go through in order to elevate love to such a height of disinterestedness that it could not become a cause for sadness. But all anguish of reciprocity is not selfish: already, when it comes to relations between human consciences, independently from any appeal to divinity, a response of indifference to goodness and sacrifice, sincere gift and a helping hand, is the sign of an ingratitude and deficiency of soul that charity cannot ignore and of which *it could not cease to suffer without ceasing to love*. This is even more evident when the one who gives himself constitutes, as the case is with God, the only possible good for this soul.

Thus we read in the Gospel that there will be more joy in Heaven for a repenting sinner than for ninety-nine just ones who have no need for penance; thus we see, also in the Gospel, the shepherd who leaves his flock to seek the lost sheep, and the housewife calling all her neighbors to share her joy in finding the lost drachma. It is remarkable that, apart from a few shades of meaning, Bergson and Péguy agree in concluding that love makes God dependent on man. One must read the admirable meditations in which the author of *Mystères de Jeanne d'Arc* (Mysteries of Joan of Arc) [Péguy], whom we could call the Bach of our literature, showed how this kind of privilege granted to the sinner comes from the fact that he had put hope and fear in the heart of God. Saint Louis trembling for the salvation of Joinville or Christ weeping on the death of Judas [sic.] do not think of affirming themselves as *apathes* (impassible) or *autarkes* (master of self).[94]

How remarkable this meeting is between Lachièze-Rey, Bergson and Péguy! The extreme precision of the text is notable: God, who creates out of his all-power—the all-power of love—makes himself through his love, dependent on man, his creature. God, in himself, does not depend on man, but love *makes him* dependent. "All this," Hans Urs von Balthasar remarks, developing the same idea, "is infinitely remote from Hegel, yet it is the truth of Hegel, but in the field of the reciprocal freedom of love."[92]

Yet, the word of Goethe remains an obsession: "If I love you, what do you care about it?" It is a cry of extreme loneliness, and of such an independent pride that the God who desires, hopes, depends and fears, seems at first remote and smaller—which is why it might be better not to avoid, but to go through the temptation of preferring Goethe to the Gospel, but not without suspecting the suspicious one! Let him confess the contempt hidden by his *hauteur*! Let him recognize that his greatness is affirmed at the cost of mine! For if it is a matter of indifference to him whether I love him or not, it means that my being is of no great importance to him! His is enough to him. Yet in a contradictory way: the one who loves is not self-sufficient.

Love, according to Goethe, escapes suffering. It is not creative. It is an *agape* without *eros* which, excluding risk, destroys itself as *agape*. If his eternal decision is such as Goethe sees it, one must say that in creating, God looks without trembling on battlefields, atomic bombs, and Western and Eastern "Gulags": man without love and his multiform degradation. Be or become as you wish, go up or down, I am God and I love you. Contrary to Goethe, Blondel spoke in a magnificent way of this "stigmatizing sympathy with which an almighty Will filled metaphysical chasms and seemingly logical impossibilities."[96] In the order of being, suffering is an imperfection. In the order of love, it is the seal of perfection.

According to reason, a perfect being is one who is subject to neither change nor limit, who is absolute: God is called the Absolute. But this concept is purely negative. One cannot say anything about the absolute, since any determination will relativize it and in so doing, annul it. Claude Bruaire, whose Schelling-inspired philosophy is deep, recalls in this connection some basic factors that are all too often neglected: "To know," he says, "presupposes an object, a definable and enunciable object. Even if we were to accept some intuitive knowledge remaining outside the boundaries of language, such a knowledge would still have to hold some determination lest it vanish into confusion and ultimately into total vacuum. And no precision, no determination is possible without relation. A relation allows for a difference needed for real distinction. This is well expressed in the simple logic of propositions and definitions, which always stipulates that one must circumscribe what is to be known, must draw its limits through differences and oppositions. But the absolute forbids any relation. Better yet, it is this very act of forbidding. Thus the absolute, or God in religious vocabulary, describes only the purely unknowable, and as far as perfection goes, that of the vacuum. Vacuum for all knowledge, which solves in its nothingness all that religions pretend to teach us about their knowledge of God."[97]

It is not in the name of such a perfection—completely negative—that one will affirm divine impassibility as self-evident. Whoever clings to the concept of the absolute is forever staying on the same spot or goes over to atheism, which is the only logical step. A perfection that would limit God, by forbidding him to want himself to be such as he wants to be, implies a contradiction: If God exists, nothing can limit him, especially not himself. He is not nailed to his own necessity. Far from being subject to himself, he wants himself as such. He tears himself eternally from nothingness by positively charging the pre-original indetermination. He is the Decision of love, of indivisibly creative love, love incarnate and crucified. Such a decision is his very act of existence: *actus purus* or *esse* of the great Scholastics. In the reality of an eternal present which is not an eternal fixity. The human mind is disoriented if it gives in here, even slightly, to a temporalizing imagination that would objectivize a before and an after. The beginning of God is without beginning, his genesis without genesis, his becoming without becoming. Whoever draws back when faced with the abysmal night of this mystery will not avoid falling into the enigma of a flat Identity. This is what Claude Bruaire deciphered best, exerting the "right to investigation" of the philosophers to cancel "the formula of the negative absolute, a basic formula of every rationalism and of its aftermath of irreligion or atheism."[98]

It seems impossible, unless we remain in the still deep ruts of Nestorianism, to place side by side a God who is impassible in himself and the suffering of the human nature of Christ. Yet, we will not say that suffering is the essence of God. The Japanese, who are more sensitive than any other people to the sacrificial aspect of divinity, affirm this expressly at times, at least if commentators can be believed. According to Kazoh Kitamori,[99] one comes close to the mystery of God through the experience of *tsurasa*. "The motion of action" in Japanese tragedy—the drama—is *tsurasa*, that is: self-sacrifice or sacrifice of a beloved one for the sake of another. Thus God, such as Christ reveals him by his death on the cross, is sacrificial Suffering in the depth of his being. God does not suffer because he loves; he loves because he suffers. Suffering is "so essential to the nature of God that it is the very source of his love." If this were not the case, God would offer us "a cheap love."

Of course, one must not harden—through excessive systematization—the thought of the Japanese theologian. Let's admit that there is a healthy reaction against a certain liberal theology, and it is quite true, we think, that the death of Christ reveals the depth of God. But we do not believe that God *is* Tragedy. He is Beatitude and wants himself to be vulnerable Love, which is quite different. If God *is*, in essence, suffering, he is subject to himself by loving us. Unless Kitamori goes so far as to think, to use again the words of Bruaire, that "he tears himself from nothingness" by wanting himself to be Suffering. It seems to me that Revelation does not authorize such an interpretation.

A school of Hindu spirituality in the XVIth and XVIIth centuries defined the absolute Being as "essential Emotion."[100] There was quite a sentimental inflation there and it seems that Kitamori does not consent to it. But the road is slippery. One feels somewhat guilty of indiscretion and almost of irreverence when one dares meditate on what could have happened on Calvary between the Father and the Son. Yet we had suggested earlier that Jesus had reached the depths of human suffering by uniting himself on the cross to the loneliness of men. He did not know—we said—that God shared his suffering: abysmal aspect of *kenosis*. But what the Father shares then is, deeper than any other suffering, the loneliness of the Son. For he knows that the Son does not know, and his love, by preventing him from intervening, reaches the apex of his power: it is literally the *All Power*. Can we think—I ask this without going any further—that each of the divine persons is suffering on

Calvary of a suffering which is not transfigured by communion? Suffering in communion is quite different from suffering in loneliness. One of the Three, the Son, suffers in loneliness: thus, near him, in him, the Father and the Spirit. Does the incarnation reveal that Love, such as it is eternally lived by God in communion, is powerful enough to be also lived in loneliness? Vulnerability would thus be at the heart of Being as supreme Power. Let us tie the sheaf of our gleanings. God is eternal Decision to love, therefore to talk, therefore to pray, therefore perhaps to suffer. These "therefores" are unpleasant if they refer to imperatives of formal logic. I do not mean them this way. They claim to owe their rigor only to the most common and humble—though reflected—experience.

LOVE—Love cancels the indetermination of the absolute without relativizing it or limiting it. It de-termines without including a term. "Its determination," Nédoncelle says, "is to be the soul of the determinations."[101] It is the positivity of the free infinite.

WORD—If love desires—of a desire which is essential to it, reciprocity—it manifests itself as such. It declares itself. Jesus Christ is this Manifestation, this declaration. A *flatus vocis*, a declaration such as the one a lover makes to his beloved, would not express God in a divine way. But the Word made flesh truly says: "Who sees me sees the Father."

PRAYER—Emanating from love and directed to freedom, the Word is Prayer. The *eros* which is immanent to the divine *agape* offers itself to the human *eros* and asks it to ennoble itself by accepting the gift that will transfigure it into a shared *agape*. In one and the same gesture, God gives himself and begs to be accepted.

SUFFERING—When love gives up the power that would impose its law, it exposes itself to refusal. There is a suffering which is familiar to man and unknown to God: that of knowing that you are not loving enough. If God suffers, it is of loving

7

too much (all the mystics stress the word *excess*). "The *myth* of God's sadness with regard to man and stemming from love for man," Berdyaev says, "*brings us closer* to the ultimate secrets." The word "myth" is ambiguous and can be misunderstood. Let us prefer "symbol": any talk about God is somehow symbolic. But "brings us closer" expresses it best: it reminds us that we cannot touch a thunderbolt without dying, and that mystery can only be perceived through the shadows of analogy.

When Ivan Karamazov interrupts his narrative of the horrible stories he has collected of tortured children and adults who enjoy seeing them weep, he asks Aliosha, who appears ill at ease: "Do you want me to stop?" "No," Aliosha says, "I want to suffer too, go on." Masochism? Everyone interprets as he wishes. For me, the face of this young man reflects the light of God. He is the living analogy, in flesh and blood.

Chapter Seven

POETRY

"And now, look at this shimmering roll unfolded before you! It is the sea among the islands. Oh moralists, why so many explanations, and theories, and threats, when we know at once that the filth in us is irreconcilable with sapphire? Let color and perfume deliver our senses instead of enslaving them! Only a purified soul will understand the smell of a rose."[102]

Alas! The moral theologian abandons the sea, the sapphire and the rose to the poets! Also, most of the time, the dogmatician. At the level of expression, it is true, the language of rationality or explanation is naturally prosaic. I am not unaware of a danger of confusion, and I remember the comment of Alquié: "Our time is undoubtedly only too prone to confuse philosophy and art. But it also confuses quite easily philosophy and the sciences."[103] All confusion hurts reality, here perhaps more than there. To unite is not to confuse. There are in the life of the soul and the mind lateral or vertical links, mysterious "correspondences" between reason, sensitivity, spirituality and taste, a reciprocal interiority of problems. If a theologian must not borrow the language of the artists, he may question the experience translated by such a language. Not that it be necessarily wider and deeper than his own, but artists tear their experience away—better than he can do—from the thick networks of usefulness that overshadow its aspects of purest gratuitousness. They light up the most real aspect of reality.

Thought has tones that conceptual precision should not prevent from being heard in this "shadow of hearing," as Valéry puts it, which is ready to perceive them with delight. Father Louis Bouyer points out that theology, when it is "faithful to its eucharistic origins," has a "lyrical and hymnic resonance"; it expresses itself "with an exalted prose at the limits of poetry," as can be seen with the great Cappadocians, especially Gregory Nazianzen.[104] But it happens that, in the name of reason, it shuts itself up to the spirit. Then, deaf to the voice of the "poetic Logos"—that every man carries hidden within himself, Cyril of Alexandria would say—it talks about God without hearing him sing, and at the same time it sentences itself to becoming incapable of even listening to the song of the world.

We know, since Bergson, what artificiality is caused by the analysis, the cutting up of "holy reality" according to the logic of convenience, and how the most elementary observation of things can be prevented by the laws unceasingly dictated by usefulness. Emergencies, adaptations, habits, classifications, subjection to the grossest forms of sensitivity: how could one in this cold light "feel" the harmony of opposites of which the world is woven, and "perceive" the agreement in God of suffering and beatitude? "One must bear chaos in oneself," said Nietzsche, "to be able to beget a dancing star." Poets free the mind from false clarity, and tear logic away from simplifications which are necessary at a certain level of rationality, but are against nature when it comes to the essential of existence. Rationality is literally inhuman: it hurts reason, as conversely fideism hurts faith. Both pretend to aim at the mystery of God, but they use the rule of analogy on the basis of a maimed reality. One starts dreaming of a glowing analogy. I mean by this an analogy which in order to fly towards God, would lean on the experience that poets and artists bring to a glow.

The sleeping faun of Mallarmé, in that afternoon which for us is still lasting—thanks to the music of Claude Debussy—receives *opposed* sensations of coolness and heat, light and shadow, chastity and passion, in the dancing of roses, the burst of grenades, the whisper of bees and the modulations of the flute. Impossible, said Francis Jammes, "to perceive a single molecule of this solar vibration!" It is blinding! If the poet has the power to create a white sun with the rainbow and the shivers of the summer garden, how much more dazzling, in the uncreated mystery, is the nuptial unity of suffering and joy! But as it is said in *Prose pour des Esseintes*, hyperbole rises only after long "roads" of "science" and "patience." Thus there is in the attentive soul a slow maturation of a sense of God beyond all opposition, a possibility of obscure insight into simplicity. Divine Simplicity is not simple, like something we simplify to make it simpler. The anthropomorphic slope becomes quite slippery here.

As one denies a poem, when one first analyzes it in the school manner and then forgets to grasp it again intuitively in the rich unity of its complexity, in the same way one denies Transcendence while pretending to aim for it, if one affirms in an entirely abstract manner the unity of the divine attributes, without questioning the experience in which the antinomies of the contingent reality are already, in a way, concretely lived. Here, art has an irreplaceable value of guidance. While logic declares that in God the opposites are "metalogically" coinciding, art realizes this coincidence. Up to a certain point only, because it is a promise which cannot be kept. But the promise would not be a promise if it were not already an anticipation. Nicholas of Cusa, in the XVth century, launched the concept of the "coincidence of the opposites," *coincidentia oppositorum*. When reasoning reason hits "the wall of coincidence," the "simple eye of intelligence" looks beyond for God. The "learned ignorance" stops demonstrating: but leaning on symbols, it sees the Being to whom non-being is not opposed, the One to whom the multiple is not opposed, the Infinitely Great to whom the infinitely small is not opposed, the Motion to which rest is not opposed. And the Cusan coined the word *possest* to evoke the power with which the act coincides.

One cannot coin *one* word in order to suggest how suffering and joy are harmonized in God, but perhaps, through the grace of a Vermeer contemplated for a long time, or at a certain precise moment of a musical composition, we can see on "the wall of coincidence" a crack that appears and a breach that opens up. "To be as serious as a dreaming child": Gaston Bachelard calls *reverie* the power to "awaken the sources." This is quite different from *dream* which, whether it be by day or night, fulfills a past desire, mostly remote and infantile; while *reverie* reaches this deep level where man is a creator in the image of God. Beyond the scleroses of habit, it brings forth reality which seems unreal, but which is rightly called surreal by the poets. "And at times I saw what man thought he saw."

It brings the mind back to itself, freeing it from the social superficiality and worldliness that stifle it. It restores in it the call to freedom and gratuitousness. Through it, the depth of things and the depth of man are united in delight. Which is why "one does not read poetry while thinking about something else. As soon as a poetic image is renewed, in only one of its features, it manifests a primeval naïvete."[105] Naïvete or nativity, both words have the same root. It comes to life itself, grasped at its source, either before reflection has caught a hold on it, or after reason has confessed its failure if the hinderances it had attempted to harmonize are logically irreducible. To quote the Dutch philosopher Van den Berg, himself quoted by Bachelard: "We *live* continuously a solution of problems that are hopeless as far as reflection is concerned."[106] When the "poetic moment" comes forth, time ceases to "flow," it "springs." The "flat horizontality" of the duration in which one event *follows* another, one sensation after another, one feeling after another, joy after pain and pain after joy—"the successive era"—"effaces itself," and everything becomes simultaneous. This "moment" is complex: there is not *one* simultaneity but numerous simultaneities that are vertically unified.

"Essentially, the poetic moment is a harmonic relation of two opposites. In the passionate moment of the poet, there is always some reason; in the reasoned refusal, there is always some passion. Successive antitheses already please the poet. But to attain delight, ecstasy, the antitheses must contract in ambivalence . . . At least, the poetic moment is the awareness of an ambivalence. But it is more because it is an excited, active, dynamic ambivalence. The poetic moment compels the being to value or devalue. In the poetic moment, the being goes up or down, without accepting the time of the world which would bring the ambivalence back to antithesis, and what is simultaneous to what is successive . . . Hence one will find the true poetic moment of a poem in all the points where the human heart can invert antitheses."

Bachelard illustrates his discourse with the "study of a small fragment of vertical poetic time"—two words only in a Baudelaire poem entitled *Recueillement* (Recollection): "Smiling regret." Here is the context:

> See the dead years leaning from the balconies of the sky, in their old-fashioned dresses; The *Smiling Regret* emerging from the depths of water; The dying Sun dozing under an arch, and like a long shroud trailing in the East, Listen my dear, listen to the sweetly walking Night.

It is the moment when "night falls asleep and stabilizes the darkness, when the hours barely breathe, when solitude in itself is already a remorse! The ambivalent poles of the *smiling regret* almost touch one another. The *smiling regret* is therefore one of the most sensitive ambivalences of a sensitive heart. It does unfold quite clearly in a vertical time since neither of these two moments, *smile* or *regret*, is anterior to the other. The feeling here is reversible or, to put it better, the reversibility of the being is *sentimentalized* here: the smile regrets and the regret smiles, the regret consoles. None of the successively expressed times is the cause of the other: this proves then that they are ill-expressed in successive time, in horizontal time. However, there is still, from one to the other, a becoming—a becoming that can be perceived only vertically, going up, with the impression that regret becomes lighter, that the soul ascends, that the phantom forgives. Then truly misery blossoms."[107]

Bachelard defines the Baudelairean "correspondence" not as a "mere transposition that would offer a code of sensual analogies," but as a "sum of the sensitive being in a single moment." But the sensitive is not purely sensitive. In this verse "where poetic moment has never been more complete":

Vast as the night and as the light

it is not a spatial vision that is suggested, but "the double eternity of good and evil." "Night and light are immobile moments, moments black or light, gay or sad, black and light, sad and gay." Following the same line of corresponding images, the philosopher will talk about the day "when he heard the plums ripen."[108] The birth of the image is "an event of the logos." It "touched the depths before moving the surface." In receiving it, "we feel its value of intersubjectivity. We know that we will repeat it to share our enthusiasm."[109] I believe that it was Alain who said, "Art is the shortest way from one heart to the other."

Thus, says Bachelard, "the realism of the unreal imposes itself. Figures are understood by their transfiguration. The word is a prophecy."[110] One can "explain the flower through the fertilizer." It is useful, and many are experts at it. Let us prefer those who breathe in its perfume, especially when one is concerned about God. Reason advises so: for Rimbaud, and for all who seek the key to being, the song of the angels is "reasonable." To awaken us to the mystery of "the coincidence of the opposites," Bachelard is undoubtedly an unsurpassed master. He teaches on the basis of the most common realities—for instance, the flame: "Why look for dialectics of ideas when we have, at the heart of a simple phenomenon, dialectics of facts, dialectics of beings? The flame is a being without mass, yet it is a strong being."[111]

Or yet, the water of a river: "The bottom of the river has also for the painter (Claude Monet) subtle surprises. At times, a single bubble comes up from the depths of the chasm: in the silence of the surface, this bubble stutters, the plant sighs, the pond moans. And the dreaming painter is drawn to pity for a cosmic misery. Is there a deep evil lying under this Eden of flowers? Should one remember with Jules Laforgue the evil of the flowery Ophelias 'and of the white nymphs in the lakes where Gomorrah sleeps'? Yes, the most smiling water, the most flowery one, in the clearest of mornings, hides a serious flaw."[112] One must read the wonderful pages in which Bachelard meditates on the masculine and feminine gender [in the French language] of words. This leads him to subtle reflections on reverie in *animus* and reverie—deeper—in *anima*.

Immutability granted to mobility: Saint-John Perse suggests the paradox when, renouncing the pleasure of past sadness, and facing the future, he says: "Rather the golden needle than the crackling of the retina."[113] The golden needle is the point of fixity of the look, the sign of a stubborn quest. Claudel would say: "Neither regret, nor memory, nor curiosity, but only the devouring duty and the trance of straight ways." The crackling is the mobile flame, the changing flame, the haste to reflect the variety of things. If nothing is immobile in the heart of mobility, everything falls apart in the soul. If nothing is mobile around the immobility, the soul is not anymore in the world.

It is on the harp that enigmas are solved in the best way (Psalm 49:5). Mozart, if one listens to him with the heart of a child, leads more efficiently to the boundaries of the mobile divine immobility. The image brought forth by his music is not the same as that of Saint-John Perse. As was well understood by one of the best interpreters of his "thought," Jean-Victor Hocquard, Mozart has several faces but only one look. The features are mobile; the gaze is "not fixed but immutable. It seems to bubble at the edge of a smile, then burn with a wild fire if the face is drawn in vehemence. But it is always the same look, always leading to love."[114]

To express what is unique in this look "which is beyond faces," Hocquard refers himself to *La pesanteur et la grâce* (Gravity and grace) by Simone Weil: " 'The weight of flesh,' she writes, 'pulls downwards, and in order to ascend one needs the wing of the spiritual quest. But this ascension (or reascension) leaves out the flesh it has to flee, and total reality becomes thus maimed because something had to be rejected.' Then the sublime question is asked: 'What wing of a second power can make us go down without gravity?' This coming down enlightens everything without sacrificing anything pertaining to inferior reality which also needs redemption. And here is a music which touches everything, even the lowest thing, to make it pure and porous to the Light. All of Mozart is there: going down without gravity."[115] Going down without gravity: the approach to the mystery of God is qualified here in a more spiritual way than with the too general words "immobility" and "motion." The miraculous music lets us "hear" how God, while becoming incarnate, remains God; how he can suffer without his beatitude being wounded; how "serenity is truer than anguish, since it is not only freedom from this anguish but absorption and cancellation of it."[116]

If one manages to get rid of the ambiguities of romanticism, it is possible to believe in a sensitive God. Indeed, he would not be "sensitive to the heart" of men if he were not, in some way, sensitive in himself. But here, all the words collapse: the *vocabulorum inopia* of which Saint Thomas[117] suffered is as total today as it was in his time. One can only refer to certain experiences of very fine emotions which do not originate in the flesh and which do not enslave the soul; on the contrary, they are linked with freedom since in order to be moved by them one must not be troubled even if the eyes moisten and the voice vibrates. There are poignant beauties. I will venture to say, in spite of common opinion, that an intellectual person who is insensitive to them, is not a serious intellectual. Delicate sensitivity is a quality of the spiritual being. Whoever desires to be invulnerable does not carry the other in himself; he sees him outside himself. The suffering of the other touches us when we touch him without remoteness. To be sensitive is to be close. The word *tact* is one of the most beautiful in the language: it has a wonderful hesitation between the physical and the moral meaning; it goes from one to the other in a back-and-forth of charity. I think about God when Lévinas tells me about this "*passivity of the being for the other* which is only possible under the species of the bread I eat and give. But for such a thing, one must first *enjoy his bread*, not to have the merit of giving it, but in order to give one's heart—to give oneself while giving. Enjoyment is an unavoidable moment of sensitivity."[118] If God were not infinite Beatitude, questioning ourselves about his Suffering would have no meaning.

Chapter Eight

SPIRITUALITY

Talking about Kierkegaard, Kafka said: "His demonstration is accompanied with enchantment. It is possible to avoid the demonstration in order to enter the world of enchantment, as it is possible to leave the enchantment to penetrate into the world of logic, but both can be stifled at the same time by smothering the third element they have become: i.e., the living enchantment, a destruction of the world which far from destroying it, builds it."[119] This third element, in Kafka's thought, was undoubtedly mystical theology under its most negative form. For us it will simply be, after reflection and its poetic extension, the spontaneity which is naively recovered. To enter the Kingdom we must be like children (Mt 18:3), but we must be on guard not to forget the words of Saint Paul: ". . . but now I am a man, and all childish ways are put behind me" (1 Cor 13:11). The spirit of childhood and the rejection of infantilism are necessary to the same degree.

It is difficult to believe in God when God is a desert. Solitude with God appeases. But solitude from God burns one to a cinder. Solitude among men is often so unbearable that one is ready to do anything in order to escape from it. God then becomes a "means" that is "used." Not God, but his false image. This is why, refusing this degradation on my behalf, he escapes. The "means" is lacking. Then God is God. He is never so much God as when I am "missing" him. But this hurts very much. This also hurts him very much. He suffers when he makes me suffer. If he wounds me, he wounds himself. To be wounded out of the duty of having to wound me is, however, his joy. It is the price of union. If I turn away, either from standing in silence before his absence, or from listlessly working to fulfill my human tasks, then I wound him with a quite different type of wound. Suffering from the pain he causes me through love, he suffers even more from the pain I deal myself through lack of love. *Pain* in another meaning, more dreadful. But his beatitude is unchangeable. "Nothing wounds God," says Angelus Silesius. "He never suffered, yet my soul can wound his heart." Paradox of transcendence which I must never cease to affirm, and which transcends itself in the vulnerability of love. The Father and the Spirit were not passive spectators of the torture of the Son. Their love was active in absence and silence. They stood at a distance, not speaking, in order to abolish any distance and communication that would have marred the perfection of union. They suffered from this suffering they had to inflict on the Just One. Wounded to have to wound him. Easter and Pentecost show that it was for the Three the highest joy, not for a period of time but in eternity.

Far from the summits, in these places close to the swamps where walking is heavy and slow, the desert is occasional. The wound is slight, quickly healed. The role of gratuitousness is infinitesimal. The suffering of God is then his patience. Given what I am, he has to prevent himself from avoiding me. He waits for the hour. It is the "patience"—*macrothumia*—of which Saint Paul talks (1 Cor 13:4). I must believe that "in the coldest miser, at the center of the prostitute and of the filthiest drunkard, there is an immortal soul saintly busy at breathing and who, being excluded during the day, practices nocturnal adoration." Even in the worldly person, even in the selfish, vain and calm accomplice of insolent inequities who is the business gangster, I must believe that "there is a sacred point saying *Pater Noster*."[120] It is more difficult than to believe in God and in his Christ. If I want to pray seriously for all of them, and without condescension, I must think—sincerity is a grace here—that I am not better than any of them. I also must, with the eyes of faith, "see" the Spirit who is in me more me than me, who is in them all more them than them all, at the same time joyful and "grieving" (Ep 4:30).

What does it mean "to love in God" those whom we cannot love "in mankind"? It means to desire that in God joy will increase and sadness decrease, and that in the same way in me, because of God, human sympathy will come forth and dislike vanish. Because of God? Will I hear again the old reproach directed against the Christians: that they do not love men for themselves? I reply that men are lovable in themselves and for themselves when the face of God, who created them in his image and semblance, is lit with joy in their presence. The highest beatitude is the most desirable and it corresponds to the noblest and finest quality of soul. But being joy of loving, it is also suffering of loving. My weakness would want to separate the two, cancel suffering and possess joy. This is not possible. How suffering is in God an element of beatitude, I pray for him to let me perceive it. At least as a remote perfume, or as a weak note coming from Eden, or as one of those "drops of the night" of which Gregory of Nyssa spoke, "that moisten the spirit with fine and obscure thoughts." It does seem that in the most parched desert the mystics, at least at times and for the space of a lightning bolt, breathe this perfume, hear this note and feel this coolness. It is sufficient for them to desire only God and to love as he loves.

When God creates—eternally for him, now for us—he knows that his Opulence becomes a desert, his Radiance a night, his Beatitude a cross. The essential of Christian spirituality is to live in the duty of the present moment of this

Paradox. This is what we run the risk of forgetting when, wanting to be Christians, we refuse to share our bread. Bread is a symbol. It is a matter of justice. There are cases in which what it demands is very clear. There are other cases in which intelligence has to make a hard, complex and long effort in order to understand factually its conditions. There is the cross of Christ. It is a beautiful thing to sing liturgically about it: it is more urgent not to displace it. The people of God expect the priest to live, in an exemplary way, "the coincidence of opposites" which makes man similar to God. There is no reason for him not to try it today as he did before. The following medieval manuscript was found in Strasbourg:

A priest must be both
Great and small,
Noble of spirit as if of royal blood,
Simple and natural as if from peasant stock,
A hero in the conquest of self,
A man who fought with God,
A source of sanctification,
A sinner forgiven by God,
Master of his desires,
A servant for the meek and the feeble,
Who does not bow before the powerful
But kneels in the presence of the poor,
Disciple of his Lord,
Head of his flock,
Beggar with wide-opened hand,
Bearer of countless gifts,
A man on the battlefield,
A mother comforting the sick
With the wisdom of age
And the trust of a child,
Aiming for the Most High

With his feet on the ground,
Made for joy,
Familiar with suffering,
Remote from all envy,
Lucid, speaking candidly,
A friend of peace,
An enemy of inertia,
Forever constant . . .
So unlike myself!

"While I was working in the factory," Simone Weil wrote, ". . . the misery of the others entered my flesh and my soul. . . . I was marked there forever with the brand of slavery, like the hot iron brand that the Romans applied to the forehead of their most despised slaves."[121] There are millions of slaves, everywhere and in all kinds of environments. The oppressing powers, be they men, things, or institutions, are refined. The masters are more enslaved than the slaves, since the selfishness that inspires the exercise of their power is the most despotic of all powers. They are more subject in their own selves than those who are subject to them. This is the universal slavery of men whom God "calls to liberty" (Gal 5:13). Verses from Baudelaire enter my prayer: "We have seen everywhere . . . the boring spectacle of immortal sin . . . Man, gluttonous tyrant, lecherous, hard and greedy. Slave of the slave and stream into the sewer . . . the poison of power enervating the despot and the people in love with the stupefying whip." My task is to free the ones and the others, according to what I am and what I can do. If God were not in me a Force of liberation, I would not believe in him. Do I need an idol?

Christ at Gethsemane drank from the chalice of slavery to the last drop. "Through his incarnation," Father Pousset writes, "he committed himself to slavery. He took the 'condition of a slave' (Ph 2:7), not only among other men, but also *with regard to God,* as a sinner. Christ lived his relationship of love with the Father in the mode of a relationship of *slave to master.* This mystery is that of the agony." At one moment, Jesus ceases to desire what the Father desires, without ceasing to be ready to "subject himself" to the will of the Master. "He assumed our condition and truly took our place: he knew the limitations of a creature and the resistance of negating wills, because this is how we relate to God when we sin: we are constrained and forced to obey; even when we bend our resisting will, we are in the condition of a slave before his master. If this is not the last word of our relationship with God, we still go through it when God's embrace becomes tighter and when sin emerges in us."

But the master-slave relationship is known by Christ only to be overcome. He is the Son: it is to the desire of the Father, and not to the will of the Master, that he responds at once. Through the master-slave relationship, he "restores the love relation between Son and Father, *by living it.*" The resurrection is the sign of this victory: the Father declares, not in words but through an act, that the Son has made him known such as he is.[122] If the Son has suffered to be the obedient slave, what can we say about the Father who consented to appear in the eyes of the Son as a Master who commands?

Simone Weil wrote: "Joy and pain are not opposed, but only the kinds of joy and pain. There are infernal joys and pains, healing joys and pains, celestial joys and pains."[123] "Not to seek not to suffer nor to suffer less, but to seek not to be altered by suffering."[124] If such an integrity is possible to man, how much more to God! "Beauty: a fruit at which we look without stretching out our hand. In the same way, a misery at which we look without drawing back."[125] "Poetry: . . . a joy which, because it is so pure and whole, is painful. A pain, which because it is pure and whole, appeases."[126] "I have spent ten days at Solesmes. . . . I had intense headaches; each sound hurt me as a blow; and an extreme effort of attention enabled me to go outside this miserable flesh, to let it suffer alone, hunched in its corner, and to find a pure and perfect joy in the incredible beauty of the chant and of the words."[127]

If I had been nailed to the cross with Christ, my side against his side, my hands against his hands, my feet against his feet, the same nails piercing him and me, our blood mingling together, would it have hurt me so much? Yes, of course: love does not prevent torn flesh from shuddering painfully. Would I have cried out? I don't know. But what a transmutation! But it is every day that one hundred million people are crucified on the five continents. If they knew Christ they might perhaps say, or try to say, with Saint Bernard: "The faithful soldier does not feel his wounds when he contemplates lovingly the wounds of his King." But I would not suggest this "consolation" if I know that I am an accomplice of those who nail their brothers to the cross.

It is not true that the dialogue of opposites is the sign of human finiteness. It is part of God's perfection. Our finiteness is rather manifested by the insufficiency or the perversion of our dialogues. We don't know how to "imitate God" (Ep 5:1) as we should. In certain quarters of the Church, people flatter themselves at times for a shallowness which is believed to be a factor of balance, while it is in fact creating divisions. We pit complemetary dualities against each other. This leads us to narrow their amplitude and ignore their depth. Thus will people oppose reflection and action, and will favor the latter at the expense of the former. Marx, whose inspiration is claimed by more than one, insisted that one is immanent to the other, and some unions remember it when they print on the first page of their bulletins: "No action without reflection; no reflection without action." In the same vein, people accept the ebb and flow of rationalism and fideism without realizing that they are responsible for these alternating and ruinous unilateralisms, insofar as they accept a problematic and superficial relationship between reason and faith. Again, in the same fashion, one clings to particulars be they individual or collective and disdains the universal unless, in the name of the group or the community, and with the excuse of reacting against a truly fatal individualism, one comes to the point where the person and his responsibility and liberty are forgotten.

At the end of the road, if we are not careful, we meet two antithetic monsters: a theology without pastoral concern, and a pastoral concern without theology. In the latter as in the former—especially in the latter—dualisms are born and multiply. False dialogues are instituted and even institutionalized at an infantile level, and bring forth the bitterest fruit: the impossibility of *any* dialogue. Sterility, division, alienation, passion, excitement at all levels, confusion of the paths: instead of overcoming what all agree to call the "crisis," people aggravate it. In order to have a deep dialogue with men, one must first dialogue seriously with oneself. It is in the heart of the person that the dualities must be unified. Fraternal encounters— which are undoubtedly one of the graces of our time—can promote silent meditation; they do not take its place. The very same Holy Spirit leads us to the desert and gathers us in the community.

Paul Claudel wrote: "Without modesty, Oh you our God, Oh Father and Mother of Israel, how you show us your way of being impassible!" "March, people of Israel! Forward, people of God! Rest was not meant for you, nor complacency on the way. God, in front of you, is suffering of these mysteries of which he is full and of which you are the only one who can relieve him. How long, through what cruel oppositions are you going to refuse him this Virgin that he claims from you, and in whose womb he longs to become incarnate? How much longer will you refuse him the cross on which he wants to go up? How much longer, says God, will you let me wait for this all-powerful word to which you well know I will be incapable of resisting? This inestimable syllable which since the creation I have been asking from your purified lips: Fiat!" "The good God whom people hurt and who cries out."[128] "The lance in the hand of Longinus went further than the heart of Christ. It opened God, it went to the very center of the Trinity."[129]

Ivan Karamazov, talking with Aliosha, evokes the legend of Saint Julian the Hospitaler: "A passer-by, hungry and cold, came one day to beg him for warmth; the saint lay on him, embraced him and started to breathe into the purulent mouth of the miserable man who was infected with a horrible disease."[130] That the mouth of God is eternally upon my purulence, how little does this certainty move me! *Purulence* is not an exaggeration: Ignatius of Loyola uses the word, and so does Fénelon. I am as certain of the infection of my breath as I am of the closeness of the breath of the Spirit. Yet my suffering is dry. This dryness is bitter to me, but the very bitterness is barely perceptible, and I hardly dare offer it as a token of my gratitude. Ivan Karamazov says that he is convinced that Julian "did that with an effort, lying to himself, with a feeling of love dictated by duty and a spirit of penance. For a man must be hidden for us to love him; as soon as he shows his face, love disappears." Other protagonists of Dostoyevsky use the same language: Stravogin in *The Possessed*, Versilov in *The Adolescent*. They are right and Saint Bernard agrees with them: "I know that a perfect knowledge of the ones and the others cannot be achieved in this world; perhaps we should not even desire it. If, as it is true, knowledge nurtures love in the heavenly life, it might harm it in this world; for who can boast of the absolute purity of his heart? True knowledge here would soon bring confusion to the one who is known, and painful surprise to the one who knows him. There will be happiness in mutual knowledge only when there will be no more stains."[131]

The warning remains true: the modern trend toward lay

or religious community must be lucid if it wants to remain healthy. "If you knew your sins, you would lose heart." Jesus Christ knows them with a perfect knowledge. Yet "I love you," he says, "more ardently than you have loved your stains."[132] The look of God on me is truly a kiss. Poets, outside of any religious feeling, have valued the power of the image: "Kissing with his eyes the forms and the colors," René Char says. Divine kiss which is at the same time creation, divinization and pardon. Kiss moist with tears. Anthropomorphism? Let anyone prefer the anthropomorphism of a dry face. I, for one, have chosen. If a mother, whose children are in pain, were to say: "I am so happy in the arms of my husband that the pain of my sons and daughters does not concern me," such a happiness would be unhappiness for her. If it comes to God, it would be absolute unhappiness. The unhappiness of being God.

An Indian mystic wrote in the XIVth century:

> He came to look for me.
> The night was dark.
> The sky was circled by heavy clouds.
> He came on this solitary path,
> Soaking with rain.
> I was there with my friends
> And I played with my childish toys.
> Alas, I did not go to meet him,
> But he came, he stayed under the trees,
> Soaking with rain.

Father Georges Morel, who quotes the text, writes: "To say that God is passible is not to project on him our own powerlessness: it is to cross, in trembling, the threshold beyond which it is finally revealed, with a tremendous clarity, that vulnerability is part of his essence, although we cannot point out to more than an imperceptible hint of its presence."[133] The Three Persons are One in being and acting, in love and beatitude; how can I believe that they are not one in suffering?

If my thought tends to this direction, Nestorius is waiting for me at the foot of the slope and so are the Docetists. For the temptation to deny that Jesus is the Word becomes then very strong. But I read in Saint John: "God loved the world so much that he gave his only Son." (Jn 3:16). By giving his Son, the Father gives somehow *more than himself*, since he is Father only for and through the Son. Jesus surrenders himself, but the Father also surrenders him. The Spirit is the kiss uniting the crucifying Father to the crucified Son.

Meditating on this mystery, I avoid of course, in spite of clumsy cliches, imagining an offended God demanding, for justice to be done, the compensation of blood poured out. Demanding has no meaning if by surrendering the Son, the Father crucifies himself. Each one of the Three Persons is crucifying and crucified. The cross of Jesus is at the heart of a Love which has eternally the form of a Sacrifice. It is identically the Beatitude of a truly One God. For love would not know perfect joy if it did not go to the very limit of itself. The Spirit is the sweet love, or the explosion of joy, on the faces of the Father and of the Son whom he unites while keeping them distinct.

If someone says that hell is a *reality*, he pretends to have about the other world information that the Christians do not have. Hell is damnation, and no one knows whether there are damned people. There is—and this is quite different—a *real possibility* inscribed at the heart of a human freedom which is respected without cheating. In one and the same indivisible act, God creates, offers his own life for sharing, and calls us to accept him. Absolute respect is interior to this act. Love would not be love, if it manipulated freedom in order to obtain reciprocity at all cost. To compel to love is not to love. What can God do but suffer, if man commits himself totally to a conscious and stubborn selfishness? We are reaching here a boundary where intelligence hesitates, abashed and disarmed.

If damnation is a terrible possibility for man, how much more for God? Why think only about myself, about us? And so little about him? In truth, dogma does not inform; it invites to an inner attitude: hope in the form of prayer. I hope for all men, without a single exception, even those who are monsters in everyone's eyes; I also hope for God. I pray to God for all; I also pray to him for him.

A prayer of Kierkegaard to obtain the intelligence of the silence of God: "Never let us forget that you speak even when you are silent; give us also this confidence, when we are waiting for your coming, that you are silent out of love as you speak out of love. Thus, whether you are silent or whether you talk, you are always the same Father, the same paternal heart, whether you guide us by your voice or ennoble us through your silence."

On Easter Sunday, 1943, Emmanuel Mounier wrote to his wife: "To experience God or not is secondary. Yet it still hurts very much, when we barely experience him." It hurts very much! Here is the word of tenderness testifying that a vigorous indifference to sensible emotion was not in Mounier the sign of a lukewarm attitude towards the living God. He saw God in men and events; he was with him in the daily achievement of his work, but he loved him—the Other whom we address. He was a man of prayer and meditation as much as a man of action. Are we moved to action by the flesh or by the spirit? In many cases, unbeknown to us, instinct is the strongest motivation. Love of others is then a form of self-love. The share of generosity which is mingled in it does not cross the threshold of disappointments. As soon as one meets failure, he withdraws. Mounier points to the criterion for discernment.

He who does not suffer is only half helping the one who suffers. We all feel this somehow, when we fear in times of pain to go to satisfied neighbors: for though neighbors, they are not close. If an emergency pushes us, we are resigned to go, but half-heartedly. We are not in agreement with ourselves *in our hearts*. When the strings of two violins are well-tuned, one sings when the other vibrates. But condescending pity, even when translated into a spontaneous and generous help, does not musically touch the soul of a suffering person. God touches us musically. Grace is vibrating. "Lord have mercy" is ambiguous. We are invoking a painfully beating heart.

Nothing can exempt us from wanting an improvement of justice and from working towards it, even if reflection and experience teach us that such a progress is and always will be ambivalent. There is a very tight knot joining the religious depth to political and social action. Here one needs great patience, in the double meaning of the word: courage or energetic reaction in the face of difficulty—*upmone* (1 Cor 13:7)—and forbearance or mildness in the pre- and post-revolutionary length of the effort—*macrothumia* (1 Cor 13:4). But patience is degraded if it is not animated by impatience. A healthy patience is an impatience which is at the same time maintained and overcome. The spiritual root of this impatience is love which could not accept the incredible slowness with which men are building a human world. But at the deeper level, at the root of the root, it is the impatience of God. When love is infinite, impatience in the face of evil is also infinite; and so also is patience. The opposites, which are mutually immanent, are eternally in dialogue.

When there are great moments of violence, imperialisms of all kinds, whether they be bloody or camouflaged, brutal actions or latent states, overt or established disorder, people are surprised by the patience of God, and it is a scandal for them. If they knew how acute, though, is God's impatience! To overcome it, no less is needed than the infinity of love. If one may imagine degrees in divine love, we will say that a lesser love impels our Father to intervene, and that a stronger love convinces him that he must efface himself in silence and absence.

This silence is the most powerful word, and this absence the most immediate presence. To doubt this, we would have to have lost our awareness of the dignity of our freedom. If God creates it, it is not in order to petrify it and substitute himself for it. The task is ours. It has to be achieved in impatience and patience.

The unity of suffering and beatitude is the secret of God. Saint Therese perceived this and desired to participate in it. That desire already started to be fulfilled in this world. Most people surely need a lengthy biblical, speculative and poetic preparation in order to appreciate the incomparable candor with which she expresses, using only simple words, what we call scholastically the "coincidence of opposites." The gift of wisdom is higher than that of intelligence, and higher yet than that of science:

"I have come to the point where I cannot suffer any more, because all suffering is sweet to me."

"Thinking about celestial happiness does not give me any joy, but I ask myself at times how it will be possible for me to be happy without suffering. Jesus undoubtedly will change my nature, otherwise I would regret the suffering and the value of tears."

"I have found happiness and joy in the world, but only in suffering, because I have suffered very much here ... Since my first communion, since I had asked Jesus to change for me all the consolations of the earth into bitterness, I had a perpetual desire to suffer. Yet, I did not think of making this into my joy; that grace was granted later to me. Until then, it was a spark hidden under the ashes or the blossoms of a tree bound to become fruit in time. But since I always saw my blossoms fall, that is, since I let myself weep when I suffered, I would tell myself in surprise and sadness: "But these will always be no more than desires!"

"The angels cannot suffer; they are not as happy as I am.

How surprised they would be to suffer and feel what I feel! Yes, they would be very surprised, because I am surprised myself!"

"I cannot think much about the happiness that awaits me in Heaven; only one thing makes my heart beat: waiting for the love I will receive and the love I will be able to give."

"I felt that on my part the soul was new. It was as if one had touched for the first time musical chords that had been forgotten until then."

These texts, for whoever knows how to read, are not in contradiction with "the ceaseless murmur of the heart."[134]

"There is joy which is the strongest."

NOTES

1. *Lumière et Vie*, No. 93, May-June 1969, p. 30.
2. Sermon 9 on the Nativity of the Lord.
3. Charles du Bos, *Choix de textes*, La Colombe, 1959, p. 81.
4. Recherches et Débats, *Semaine des Intellectuels Catholiques*, 1968, "Qui est Jésus-Christ?", Desclée de Brouwer, 1968, p. 188.
5. Christos Yannaras, *De l'absence et de l'inconnaissance de Dieu*, with a foreword by Olivier Clément, Ed. du Cerf, 1971, p. 39.
6. *Note conjointe*, Pléiade, Prose II, p. 1452.
7. Positions et Propositions II, *Oeuvres complètes*, Vol. XV, Gallimard, 1959, p. 308.
8. *Deuxième Élégie* XXX, Gallimard, 1955, p. 11.
9. Essentially, I am inspired here by a page of Father Édouard Pousset published in *Études* (September 1967, pp. 266-268) which was further developed in *Un chemin de la foi et de la liberté* (4, montee de Fourvière, Lyon, 5th), 1971.
10. *La philosophie et l'esprit chrétien*, Presses Universitaries de France, 1944, Vol. 1, p. 56.
11. *Spiritual Canticle*, exposition on stanza 7.
12. *Oeuvres complètes*, Pléiade, pp. 443-447.
13. Claudel, *Oeuvres en prose*, Pléiade, p. 627.
14. *Ibid.*, p. 1019.
15. *Ibid.*, p. 1017.
16. *Ibid.*, p. 437.
17. *De Potentia*, q. 7, art. 5, ad. 14
18. *Contra Gentes*, I, 30, end.
19. See *Le Désir de Dieu*, Aubier, 1956, p. 353 ff.
20. See *Le Seigneur*, Alsatia, 1945, Vol. II, pp. 21-29, 69-73.
21. Romano Guardini, *Le monde et la personne*, Editions du Seuil, 1939, p. 41 ff.
22. *Le pur et l'impur*, Flammarion, 1960, p. 271.
23. *Les deux sources de la morale et de la religion*, Alcan, 1932, p. 249.
24. See Henri de Lubac, *La foi chrétienne*, Aubier, 2nd ed., 1970, p. 165.
25. *Le pélerin chérubinique*, III, p. 202.
26. Jacques Pallard, *Profondeur de l'âme*, Aubier, 1954, p. 131.
27. *Deuxieme Elegie* XXX, Gallimard, 1955, p. 134.
28. "Profanation and Sanctification of Time," *Journal musical*, Desclée de Brouwer, 1966, p. 18.
29. *Bernanos par lui-même*, Ed. du Seuil, 1954, Coll. "Ecrivains de toujours."
30. Research and Debates, *Semaine des Intellectuels catholiques*.
31. Gabriel Madinier, *Conscience et Mouvement*, Presses Universitaries de France, 1938, pp. 173-175.
32. Jacques Guillet, unpublished lecture.

33. Rimbaud, *Oeuvres complètes*, Pléiade, 1954, pp. 269-273.
34. Edouard Pousset, *op. cit.*, p. 93.
35. See Jean Wahl, *Petite histoire de l'existentialisme*, ed. Club Maintenant, 1947, pp. 84 and 90.
36. *Adversus haereses*, V, 18, 3 coll. "Sources chrétiennes," No. 153, p. 244.
37. *Les Ages de la vie spirituelle*, Desclée de Brouwer, 1954, p. 44.
38. Karl Rahner, *Ecrits théologiques*, vol. 8, Desclée de Brouwer, 1967, p. 125.
39. Hans Urs von Balthasar, *La Gloire et la Croix*, vol. 1, Aubier, 1965, p. 25.
40. *Agenda 1948*, 21, 23 and 24 January. See Béguin, *op. cit.*, p. 146.
41. Charles du Bos, *Choix de textes*, La Colombe, 1959, p. 236.
42. C. H. Dodd, *Le fondateur du christianisme*. Ed. du Seuil, 1972, p. 55.
43. *Journal d'un curé de campagne*, Pléiade, pp. 1192-1194.
44. Henri de Lubac, *Paradoxes*. Ed. du Seuil, 1959, Foreword.
45. *Ibid.*, p. 13.
46. *Profondeur de l'âme*, Aubier, 1954, p. 152.
47. *Revue Thomiste*, 1969, I.
48. Claude Bruaire, *La raison politique*, Fayard, 1974, p. 261.
49. Albert Camus, *L'homme révolté*, Gallimard, 1951, p. 53.
50. See *Les hommes devant l'échec*, published under the management of Jean Lacroix, P.U.F., 1968, pp. 141-161.
51. *Dieu en quête de l'homme, Philosophie du judaïsme*. Ed. du Seuil, 1968, p. 150.
52. André Neher, *L'essence du prophétisme*, P.U.F., 1955, p. 95.
53. *Axes*, February-March 1975, p. 9.
54. *Exercices spirituels*, No. 206.
55. Jacques Guillet, *Jésus-Christ dans notre monde*, Desclée de Brouwer, 1974, p. 63.
56. J. Guillet, *op. cit.* p. 71.
57. Julien Green, *Oeuvres complétes*, Pléiade, 1973, Vol. II, p. 27.
58. *Parochial and Plain Sermons*, Vol. III, No. 10.
59. Paul Claudel, *Cinq grandes Odes, La maison fermée*.
60. Marcelle Lévy, *Cahiers universitaries catholiques*, Qui est notre Dieu?, 1967, p. 112.
61. Paul Valéry, *Le cimetière marin*.
62. *Ibid*.
63. René Char, *Recherche de la base et du sommet*, Gallimard, 1955, p. 103.
64. Paul Claudel, *L'épée et le miroir*, Gallimard, 1939, p. 65.
65. *Homélies sur Ezéchiel*, 6, 6.
66. Henri de Lubac, *Histoire et esprit, L'intelligence des Ecritures d'après Origène*, 1950, pp. 241-243.
67. *Sur le Cantique des Cantiques*, sermon 26, n. 5, Translated by A. Béguin.
68. H. de Lubac, *op. cit.*
69. *Summa Theologica*, I a, q. 21, art. 3.
70. Jacques Maritain, *loc. cit.*
71. *Journal*, Plon, 1938, Vol. I, p. 18.
72. Maurice Nédoncelle, *La pensée religieuse de Friedrich von Hügel*, Vrin, 1935, pp. 130-133. See F. von Hügel, *Essays and Addresses in the Philosophy of Religion*, London, 1926.
73. Aubier, 1942, p. 285.
74. Quoted by Xavier Tilliette, *Schelling, Une philosophie en devenier*, Vrin, 1970, Vol. II, p. 443.
75. Paul Claudel, *Journal*, Pléiade, 1969, Vol. II, p. 14.

76. Paul Valéry, *Air de Sémiramis*.
77. Jean Lacroix, *Le désir et les désirs*, P.U.F., 1975, p. 165.
78. Fondation et Association Teilhard de Chardin, cahier VII, *Sens humain et sens divin*, Ed. du Seuil, 1971, p. 95-97.
79. See Jean Meyendorff, *Introduction á l'étude de Grégoire Palamas*, Ed. du Seuil, 1959, pp. 292, 306 ff.
80. Olivier Clément, Preface to C. Yannaras, *De l'absence et de l'inconnaissance de Dieu*, Ed. du Cerf, 1971. pp. 25, 14.
81. H. Urs von Balthasar, *Le mystère pascal*.
82. *Summa Theologica*, I a, q, art. 7; *Contra Gentes*, II, 12-14.
83. *Victor-Marie comte Hugo*, Pléiade, Prose II, pp. 730, 734. See F. Varillon, *Etudes*, June 1973, p. 870.
84. Karl Rahner, *Problèmes actuels de christologie*, Desclée de Brouwer, 1965, p. 24.
85. *Journal*, Vol. I, p. 20.
86. *Les Complaintes, Préludes autobiographiques*.
87. *Oeuvres complètes*, Pléiade, 1945, p. 49.
88. *Nouvelle Revue théologique*, June 1932, "Une philosophie du devoir."
89. See Jean Lacroix, *op. cit.*, p. 65.
90. Paul Claudel, *Cantate a trois voix, Cantique du coeur dur*.
91. 1 Jean Lacroix, *op. cit.*, p. 79.
92. *Ibid.*, p. 145.
93. See Fernand Guimet, "*Caritas ordinata* and *amor discretus* in the trinitarian theology of Richard of Saint-Victor," in *Revue du Moyen Age latin*, August-October 1948.
94. Pierre Lachéze-Rey, *Le Moi, le monde et Dieu*, Aubier, 1950, pp. 130-132.
95. H. Urs von Balthasar, *La Gloire et la Croix*, II, *Styles* Vol. II, Aubier, 1972, p. 363.
96. *Letters philosophiques de Maurice Blondel*, Aubier 1961, p. 232.
97. Claude Bruaire, *Le droit de Dieu*, Aubier, 1974, p. 18.
98. *Ibid.*, pp. 107-108.
99. *Theology of the Pain of God*, 1946. See *Concilium* No. 95, pp. 64 ff.
100. See André Ravier, *La mystique et les mystiques*, Desclée de Brouwer, 1965, p. 794.
101. Maurice Nédoncelle, *Vers une philosophie de l'amour*, Aubier, 1946, p. 101.
102. Paul Claudel, *L'oiseau noir dans le soleil levant*, Gallimard, 1929, p. 127.
103. Ferdinand Alquié, *Philosophie du surréalisme*, Flammarion, 1955, p. 8.
104. Louis Bouyer, *Le Fils éternel*. Ed. du Cerf, 1974, p. 353.
105. Gaston Bachelard, *La poétique de la rêverie*, P.U.F., 6th ed. 1974, p. 3.
106. *La poétique de l'espace*, P.U.F., 8th ed., 1974, p. 11.
107. *Le droit de rêver*, P.U.F., 3rd ed., 1973, pp. 224-232.
108. *L'air et les songes*, Jose Corti, 1943, p. 63.
109. *La poétique de l'espace*, p. 7.
110. *L'air et les songes*, p. 13.
111. *La flamme d'une chandelle*, P.U.F., 1968, p. 20.
112. *Le droit de rêver*, p. 12.
113. Saint-John Perse, *Vents, Oeuvres complétes*, Pléiades, 1972, p. 227.
114. Jean-Victor Hocquard, *La pensée de Mozart*, Ed. du Seuil, 1958, p. 220.
115. *Ibid.*, p. 620. See Simone Weil, *La pesanteur et la grâce*, Plon, 1947, pp. 5, 197.
116. *Ibid.*, p. 221.
117. *Summa Theologica*, I a, q. 37. art. 1.
118. Emmanuel Lévinas, *Autrement qu'être ou au-delà de l'essence*, Martinus Nijhoff, Haagen, 1974, p. 91.

119. Franz Kafka, *Gesammelte Schriften*, Vol. VI.
120. Paul Claudel, *Conversations dans le Loir-et-Cher (Oeuvres en prose*, Pléiade, 1965), p. 731.
121. Simone Weil, *Attente de Dieu*, La Colombe, 1950, p. 74.
122. Edouard Pousset, "L'Agonie: le passage du Christ par la relation maitre-esclave," in *Annoncer la mort du Seigneur*, Profac, Lyon.
123. *La pesanteur et la grâce*, p. 109.
124. *Ibid.*, p. 106.
125. *Ibid.*, p. 197.
126. *Ibid.*
127. *Attente de Dieu*, p. 75.
128. *Commentaires et exégèses, Oeuvres completes*, Gallimard, 1974, Vol. XXVII, pp. 18, 29, 69.
129. *L'epée et le miroir*, Gallimard, 1939, p. 256.
130. Dostoyevsky, *Les Frères Karamazov*, Book V, Ch. 4.
131. Quoted by Henri de Lubac, *le drame de l'humanisme athée*, Spes, 4th ed., 1950, p. 295, note 5.
132. Pascal, *Le mystère de Jésus*.
133. See *Christus*, No. 83, June 1974, pp. 311-312.
134. Ps 19:15.